Pı
by Glenn Edwards and Jordan Edwards

"...a great book to keep as a resource and read over and over again. As an entrepreneur you constantly need encouragement and reminders on how to stay excited about business opportunities. There are so many aspects of a business and this book touches on all of them. Would recommend to those at all levels including high school and college students."

"If you have ever had a great business idea but we're unsure of where and how to start, or whether you should really pursue it in the first place, this book not only provides great insight and advice, but motivates you to get started. The authors speak from experience and really know what they are talking about. Highly recommend!"

"...incredibly insightful [book that] offered useful tips for not only the first-time entrepreneur but even for those who have been in business for a long time."

Business Jiu Jitsu

Discover the Entrepreneur's Path
through the Wisdom of Jiu Jitsu

Jordan Edwards

Business Jiu Jitsu
© Copyright 2024 by Jordan Edwards

Paperback ISBN 978-1-964014-16-6
Hardback ISBN 978-1-964014-17-3
Ebook ISBN 978-1-964014-18-0

Published by Tasfil Publishing, LLC
New Jersey, USA

In the pages of this book, you will find wisdom shared by many extraordinary individuals. These insights come from ADCC world champions like Gordon Ryan, esteemed coaches such as John Danaher, Olympians including Jimmy Pedro and Travis Stevens, billion-dollar CEOs like Rich Byrne, Navy SEAL and special operations veterans like JP Dinnell and Nick Koumalatsos, and other world-class guests who have graced my Business Jiu Jitsu podcast with their profound knowledge.

However, I dedicate this book, Business Jiu Jitsu, to three people who have influenced me profoundly—more than any other mentors I have had, living or past.

My father, Glenn, as been my greatest mentor in both life and business.

My sensei, Nardu Debrah, selflessly dedicates himself to his students and to the practice of martial arts.

And my wife, Danielle, who exemplifies goodness and grit and embodies the philosophy I strive to impart through these pages.

This book is for my children, Axel, Mac, and Baby I, who, at the time of this writing, we eagerly anticipate joining our family soon.

"If you know the way broadly, you'll see it in everything."
– Miyamoto Musashi, *A Book of Five Rings*

Table of Contents

A Note from the Author

The stories and people in this book are all real. It is not my intention to hurt or disparage anyone; therefore, some names have been changed to protect the people or sensitive information.

Many of these stories have been condensed (to protect your reading time), and others are pulled solely from my memory, so there may be slight inaccuracies. I've included these stories to illustrate the decisions I made in the past and how they influenced my future. They are not meant to be a full, historic, or accurate retelling; however, I have made sure to be as open and honest as possible (even when it paints me in a bad light).

This is not a get-rich-quick book. The tools and techniques I teach in this book will take years of hard work, discipline, and study—they took me over a decade to learn myself. If you're just starting out or at the midway point in your journey, please don't compare yourself to me now. I have made many mistakes, and all of them have helped me get to where I am today. (Many of them are detailed in this book.)

In both life and business, you have to learn how to

enjoy these lessons, even when they're hard, even when they hurt, even when there's blood, sweat, and tears—a lot of tears. I guarantee that you will find blood, sweat, and tears in life and in this book.

Introduction

I am the CEO of a fashion company, yet my biggest deficit in my business is having no background in fashion. I am, instead, a businessperson. But that's not all I am. Often, our greatest weaknesses can become our superpowers.

For over a decade, jiu jitsu was my secret identity. My business and my passion never crossed. I couldn't find a place for them to intersect—until I did. In 2019 I created the *Business Jiu Jitsu* podcast, where I began to explore the connection between the principles of business and jiu jitsu by interviewing experts in both. I was able to bring my two worlds together and have one life.

The idea of *Business Jiu Jitsu* came from conversations with my teammates. After training, my teammates would often come up to me with a business idea. "I want to leave law enforcement and start a fashion business," or "I want to open a gym," or "I want to flip a house." We would begin to talk about how to launch and run a business, but I would use jiu jitsu metaphors because the language of business was foreign to them.

At the beginning of both your jiu jitsu journey and your business journey, you're so naive that you don't know what you don't know. As a matter of fact, if you knew what you didn't know, you probably wouldn't take the first step because the journey might feel overwhelming. That's the blessing and the curse of being a beginner in anything. The fact that you don't know how hard it is makes you willing to do it.

When I started my podcast, I had no connections. I didn't have an Instagram account. I had never had a podcast. I didn't have a microphone. I hadn't recorded anything before. But I had enough life and business experience to know that when I wanted to do something, I needed to just start. I asked one of my lifelong best friends, Jon Friedman, to join me, and we recorded.

In the past, if I'd wanted to start a podcast, I would've spent weeks or months researching starting a podcast. I would have thought, *I need to set up the perfect microphone. What one does Joe Rogan use? How do I edit video? What software do I need?* But with more than ten years of running businesses under my belt, I knew that the only thing that I really needed to do was go record a podcast. The act of actually starting my podcast became the essence of what *Business Jiu Jitsu* actually is: the alchemy of just starting and using my attributes and collections of experiences (i.e., muscle memory) to succeed.

By making the podcast, I've had the privilege of talking to the best minds in Brazilian jiu jitsu, the best coaches, world champions, Navy Seals, Olympians, billion-dollar CEOs, and more. Throughout this book, I include wisdom learned from these conversations, occasionally quoting them directly.[1]

Guests on the Business Jiu Jitsu Podcast include:

Randy Brown	Jonathan Friedman	Deborah Gracie
Rich Byrne	Greg Melita	Nur Khan
Jon Thomas	Zachary Lipari	JJ Winans
Mike Conicelli	Dan Silvert	Jimmy Pedro
Paul Karger	Simona Adrejic	Mike Constantiner
Casey Pedro	Travis Stevens	Will Harris
Arthur Abrams	Gordan Ryan	Michael Zenga
John Danaher	Elliot Bayev	Daniel Moskowitz
Ricardo Almeida	Neil Shoney	Freddy Trillo
Brian Edwards	Zach Maslany	Placido Santos
JW Wright	Jason Khalipa	Nick Koumalatsos
Craig Hanaumi	Robert Drysdale	Riccardo Ammendolia
Kit Dale	Damien Anderson	John Clarke
Colton Crawford	Thalys Pontes	Jamie Giovinazzo
Alexander Darwin	Pete Roberts	Sophie Shap
Chris Matakas	Tim Hennessey	Jarrell Garcia
Kyle Cerminara	Chris Martinez	Ben Kovacs
JP Dinnell	Niamh Ross	Mike Rodgers
Kyle Rodgers	Shane Sorensen	Dave Crull
Glenn Edwards	Frank Rosenthal	Patrick Donabedian
Rick Bookstaber	Ari Goldman	Shawn Ambrosino
Adelita Montero	Matt Culley	

---

[1] You can find and listen to Business Jiu Jitsu on your favorite podcast platform.

Why the Intersection of Jiu Jitsu and Business?

In our day-to-day lives, we're classified even when we don't want to be classified. We're grouped by race, religion, and socioeconomic status. It's extremely difficult to break out of these tropes. It can be hard to go outside of your community—whether that's a synagogue, church, religious group, or even friendship circle—and find meaning. The beauty of jiu jitsu is it's a path you choose, just like you can choose the entrepreneurial path. You enter a new world where your own attributes, the things that are unique to you, can either be your greatest weapons or your biggest deficits.

The process of being an entrepreneur is very lonely and very difficult. There's no single playbook on the right way to start a business. Yes, there are countless business books on how to start a business, how to run a business, how to fundraise, how to market, and more, but there's no one right way that's guaranteed. You have to carve your own entrepreneurial path.

In the same way, there's no one way to do jiu jitsu. A joke we like to tell in the dojo is that if you ask ten black belts how to do an armbar, a basic fundamental technique, you'll get ten different answers.

Yet both of these paths teach you how to deal with adversity in such a way that no matter what comes at you, you can figure out how to keep moving. Contrast that against the average person: when adversity hits, they freeze. They don't have the answer. They don't know what to do, and either life or an attacker is going to overwhelm them.

This book is about the intersection of these two paths. Throughout these pages, I'll show you how the lessons I learned over fourteen years of practicing jiu jitsu, as well as fifteen years of business experience, helped me make the best possible business decisions and maneuvers for Mixology Clothing Company during one of the hardest times for business owners: the 2020 COVID-19 global pandemic. The core insight I aim to impart through this book is the methodology and rationale behind effective decision-making in business.

The Art of Problem-Solving

Problem-solving is an art, and performing under pressure is very difficult. Imagine that you're asked to solve a Rubik's cube sitting in your chair at home. Sounds doable, right? Especially with quick access to YouTube and Google in your pocket. Now imagine you have to solve it after running three miles at a dead sprint with your life on the line. The pressure has changed something simple into an entirely different scenario.

Learning how to perform under pressure is one of the greatest skills that jiu jitsu can teach you. But you have to start with the fundamentals.

It's hard to feel that you're getting better when you first start jiu jitsu—or even that you've learned anything at all. For the first three to six months, beginners can often feel beaten down until something magical happens: somebody newer than them comes in for their first class.

It's as if they have gained an absolute superpower over the other person because just a few months of training compared to no training makes a huge difference. They realize they've learned more than they had thought. This is what keeps many people on the path of jiu jitsu.

There's a series of fundamental principles of fighting that we'll discuss throughout the book that help you survive in jiu jitsu. But what's also incredible is that, metaphorically, many of these same principles manifest in the business world too.

> The idea of lineage is very important in jiu jitsu. So for my jiu jitsu readers, my lineage goes:
>
> the Gracie Family > Renzo Gracie > John Danaher > Nardu Debrah (my sensei) > me.

My sensei, Nardu Deborah, has an after-class ritual at Budokan Martial Arts Academy. We call it a mat chat, which is when Sensei discusses the high-level philosophy of what we were learning that day in physical training.

When growing my career as a young entrepreneur and then a young president of a business on my way to becoming a CEO, I often encountered problems that I didn't have the answers to.

A pivotal moment happened in my life when I met with the legendary private equity investor Keith Miller, one of the founding members of Goode Partners, about the possibility of him investing in my business, Mixology Clothing Company. Toward the end of what felt like a fantastic meeting in his beautiful office, he began grilling me with questions about my business. The problem was I didn't know any of the answers to his questions. After he was done, he looked me dead in the eyes and said a line that altered the course of my life: **"Jordan, you're a nice guy, but you don't know enough about your business."**

When I walked out of that meeting, I had two options. I could say, "Fuck him. He doesn't know what he's talking about. I'm the shit. I grew this business." Or option two, I could choose to learn. Thankfully, I had already started my jiu jitsu journey, so I understood the value of both tapping out and choosing to continue to learn. I chose to learn.

> A quick definition: tapping out (or tapping) is the voluntary submission to an opponent, meaning you acknowledge they have bested you. We'll talk in more detail about the importance of tapping throughout the book.

I wrote down all the questions he asked me and put them on my corkboard in my office, so I'd see them every day. (I still have them today, only now they're framed on my wall as a reminder to keep a beginner's mindset and seek the path of learning, always.) Then, I started finding the answers to all those simple, basic business questions.

In business, the answers you seek are at your fingertips should you decide to open up one of the many hundreds of thousands of incredible business books that leaders, investors, generals, athletes, coaches, and other experts have written. I have been more grateful to the mentors that I found on the pages of books than I ever could have imagined because the answers to so many problems that I faced were always there when I needed them. The only thing I had to do was open the books and read (or listen to) them. The value I've received from books is a large part of my inspiration for writing this book. I am always shocked at how honest, open, candid, and helpful the leaders in these books are. I also want to pass on what I have learned and experienced to others, which has the added benefit of solidifying my own technique.

Jordan and the Birth of Mixology Clothing Company

I'm Jordan Edwards. I'm a partner at Chart Organization, my family's investment business. We have investments in commercial real estate, security, water management, technology companies, and direct-to-consumer companies. I'm also the CEO of Mixology Clothing Company, a business my sister Gabrielle and I run together and one of our seed investments that has grown into a beautiful tree.

In early 2002, at thirteen, Gabrielle began working for a small boutique down the street from our home called Beautiful Girl, which was run by a young couple, Jon and Renee Shapiro. She worked there all through middle school and high school and into college.

My sister was in college when the 2008 recession hit, and the Shapiros started to lose their business. They were forced to put their whole inventory at 90 percent off just to pay the bills. Jon, who would become my (now former[2]) business partner, realized that women were lining up to buy the clothes at discounted prices. Looking into this trend further, he noticed that the fashion market had shifted toward buying both designer statement pieces, like Chanel and Hermes, *and* fast fashion, like H&M and Zara. Yet most small boutiques didn't offer these fast fashion price points. This led to the idea and name for Mixology Clothing Company, a boutique that mixed and matched price points and styles.

Knowing our father was a local business fixture, Jon asked him for an investment to fund this new concept. My dad said, "Sounds like a great idea, but I have no interest in the fashion retail business." My mom, Lisa, however, reminded him that if he didn't help, this young couple with three young kids would lose everything—the same young couple that had treated my sister like a daughter during her formative years. Gabrielle had found her home and calling in fashion. So my dad agreed to a $50,000 investment in the very first Mixology Clothing Company store in Oceanside, New York.

To my dad's amazement, within the first three

---

[2] Jon retired from the fashion industry and since then, the Edwards family has had 100 percent control of Mixology Clothing Company.

months, during the darkest days of the recession, Jon returned my dad's initial investment. The seed of Mixology Clothing Company was born and grew rapidly over the next decade—despite a rough patch during Hurricane Sandy that we'll discuss in Chapter 1.

From 2009 to 2019, there were a lot of ups and downs with many hard-fought lessons won. Throughout this book, we'll follow Mixology's journey through COVID, as well as the decisions I made in real time that helped Mixology's survival and growth in the face of extreme adversity. Those decisions were only possible because of all the times I metaphorically tapped out in the years before.

It's important for you to know I have messed up a lot. I have made mistakes of every kind. I have failed. I have looked stupid in front of colleagues, family, and friends. Those same friends, employees, and partners have mocked me both to my face and behind my back. Failures that aren't followed up by resounding success and the constant small jabs by the people around you are the stories you rarely find on Instagram, LinkedIn, headlines, press releases, or magazine articles.

But my greatest decisions only came after repeated mistakes. I had to learn from my failures—and sometimes through the pages of books like this one. As is often said, it takes ten years to make an overnight success. As this book unfolds and you hear me discuss the physical, technical, tactical, and mental principles I use to win, remember that I, too, was once a business and jiu jitsu white belt. I once knew nothing and made the wrong decisions. Failure is only true failure when you don't learn from it.

Throughout this book, I'll refer to my "technical framework." It refers to the learned behavior I brought with me from jiu jitsu to business. It's a lifetime pursuit of refining fundamentals, or as the Japanese call it, kaizen: daily improvement for the better.

In each jiu jitsu class, you are taught a set of techniques, and then you drill them and use them in live sparring. At the end of each class at Budokan Martial Arts Academy, you return to center for the mat chat, where you discuss what you have learned in a larger context, bringing it into focus on the big picture. It wasn't long before I realized I needed to bring this technical framework to my business world (and eventually to my personal life as well).

I started to take an aggressive approach to reading books to increase my knowledge, and I also started taking business classes. For example, most people think that because they took an accounting course in college, they never have to do it again. But what jiu jitsu taught me was that I can learn and practice the same technique dozens of times and still be bad at it.

Most of the people I know are lucky if they read a handful of books a year or if they have taken one class since college. I've taken dozens of leadership seminars and courses in the fifteen years since I graduated college, and in 2022, I earned my Executive MBA. I've also read hundreds of books on business, history, philosophy, and more.

During my EMBA studies, I enrolled in accounting for the third time, adhering to Warren Buffet's belief that "accounting is the language of business." Each experience deepened my understanding of accounting, particularly the latest one, after managing a business for over fifteen years with a dedicated accounting department and an external auditing firm. This time, my grasp of accounting was significantly enhanced compared to before, and I was able to speak the "language" in a way I hadn't previously.

That's the beauty of this technical approach. It's actively going out and putting yourself in a position to recognize that you need to keep polishing your skills and practicing continuous learning to gain a deeper understanding each time you revisit a topic or technique.

This Book

This book is broken into three parts: Learning the Basics, Controlling Your Thoughts, and Combining Your Knowledge.

In Learning the Basics, shit has hit the fan, and everything is going wrong. All your plans are not panning out, and you feel the weight of the world on your shoulders. First, you need to learn how to create some space so you can breathe. With space, you can recover your guard so you can move into an offensive position. Just be sure that you don't go too hard too fast, or else you'll run out of energy.

In Controlling Your Thoughts, fear and failure are getting to you. Your friends, your family, your network: they could be your greatest source of encouragement, or they could be your biggest detractors (likely both). In the end, however, you're only really competing with yourself.

In Combining Your Knowledge, it's time to get vulnerable and start taking risks. Without risk, there is no reward. Yet you need to be calculated in your risk-taking by putting a system of controls in place. These will give you the leverage you need to win. Once the fight is done, your job isn't over. You need to keep training so you can continue to get better every day.

I'll teach these concepts through a three-step format. Each chapter will examine a jiu jitsu principle, discuss the 2020 Mixology Clothing Company journey, and end with a mat chat that brings the jiu jitsu and business concepts together.

By the end of the book, you'll understand how jiu jitsu can make you a better entrepreneur by helping you make strategic, technical business decisions during times of uncertainty and fear.

Part One

Chapter 1
Creating Space

A few years after I graduated from college, I went to Fire Island with a big group of friends. It was a time in our lives when everyone was still single, and we rented a house on the beach to party.

Fire Island is a barrier beach located off the south shore of Long Island, New York. To get to the island, you have to take a ferry. Once there, there are no cars. You have to walk or bike everywhere, including to the downtown area where all the bars and clubs are located.

Every day was a massive party on the beach. If I looked left, it was people I knew as far as I could see. If I looked right, it was people I knew as far as I could see. I could walk up and down the beach and keep running into friends. Everywhere I stopped, someone would offer me a drink. We were having the time of our lives.

I was still trying to relive the glory years of my athletic days. Like most of the days spent on the beach, we were jumping in the water, fighting the waves, and body surfing. But a few days into the trip, we had the roughest ocean conditions I had ever seen. Compound that with the fact we had been drinking the day and night before, and the whole day so far, and I found myself caught by a strong current that pulled me under and out.

Before I knew it, I was under the surface and felt like I was drowning. I pulled with everything I had, kicking my legs and swinging my arms, but no matter what I did, I couldn't feel control. I thought, *I'm going to die.*

As that bleak thought crossed my mind, I felt sand under my fingers. I said to myself, *You're not going to be the asshole who dies in front of every person you've ever met.* I literally pulled myself to shore using the sand and kicking as hard as I could. By the time I pulled myself out of the water, I had zero energy left. I was overwhelmed with a feeling of complete helplessness—of being overwhelmed, drained, and embarrassed.

When I looked up, I was over one hundred yards from where I had started. I lay there, taking big, deep breaths to get myself back together. I finally stood up and walked back over to my friends, thinking, *Thank god I didn't die.* Not one minute later, one of my dear friends had to get pulled out of the ocean by lifeguards and almost died the same way I had.

That was the closest brush with death that I've ever had. It's a feeling you can't replicate until you've felt like you have the weight of the world on your shoulders.

Jiu Jitsu Principle: Making Space to Escape

When I was in college, I started watching the UFC and got very into their reality show, *The Ultimate Fighter*, on FX. A few years out of college and no longer competing in sports, I was looking for a way to get back into shape. I chose jiu jitsu thanks to one of my best family friends, Ryann Levine (now Ryann Lorberbaum). Her father, Lou, was a lifelong martial artist and, at the time, was training mixed martial arts fighters.

Over the years, I had trained in some martial arts with Lou in his basement.[3] He would show me some techniques, and we would practice them. At half my size, he would throw me around like a rag doll. One time he gave me a ten-inch plastic training knife and said, "Try to get this knife to touch my skin." No matter what I did, I couldn't get the plastic blade to touch him. Every thrust or slash ended the same way: with me on my back.

I ran into Ryann and her father one night at dinner, and I asked if we could meet up for some training. I was looking for a good way to lose some weight, get active, and stay healthy. He replied, "I'm opening a jiu jitsu academy. You should come down and train."

When I agreed, I never imagined that I would fall in love with the art. I agreed in the same way people join

---

[3] As it would turn out, there were many other legends who would train in that basement, including my sensei Nardu Debrah, UFC champion Matt Serra and his brother Nick, Rodrigo Gracie, and many more.

19

the gym. I didn't have grand ambitions of being a fighter. I simply wanted an activity to do and knew I liked the UFC.

It was very clear from my first class how little I knew about the sport.

When you begin doing jiu jitsu, there are several fundamental techniques that you need to learn in order to become competent. Frequently, when people who think they can fight (the ones who call themselves "street fighters")—and even people who have done other martial art forms their whole lives—start at jiu jitsu and train with people who started learning only six months before them, they think their partner has a superpower.

It's not a superpower but a measure of control that the jiu jitsu fighter can assert over the newcomer. I've often heard people say when watching videos of jiu jitsu fights, "Why don't they just stand up? Why not just push the other person out of the way?" It's not that simple. Many jiu jitsu techniques and positions are similar to a boa constrictor: the more you move, the tighter the position becomes.

The first techniques you learn in jiu jitsu are a specific set of movements: bridging, shrimping, technical get-ups, the art of falling, hitting the ground, and eggbeaters, which is rotating your legs and hips. All of these have the same purpose: to teach you how to make and take space from your opponent. What surprises many newcomers is that there is an art to making and taking space.

Rich Byrne is a Brazilian jiu jitsu black belt under

John Danaher (one of the best coaches in the world), a Master Gi, and a Nogi World Champion. Rich is also the former CEO of Deutsche Bank, the current president of Benefit Street Partners (a $76 billion asset management firm), a former marathon runner, and in his early sixties. When Rich came on the podcast, he told me about his journey into the sport.[4]

As Rich's running career was coming to an end because his knees couldn't handle it anymore, he decided to move to jiu jitsu. Rich is a high performer. He's been at the top of his profession his entire career, and he seeks excellence in everything he does.

He was also the banker for the Fertitta brothers when they bought and grew the UFC. When you're the banker to the owners of the UFC, you get access to some of the best people in the sport. When Rich mentioned wanting to take private lessons in jiu jitsu, the Fertitta brothers connected him with Renzo Gracie, one of the most legendary fighters of all time and owner of one of the best associations with dozens of affiliate schools all over the world.

When Rich took his first lesson at Renzo Gracie Academy, he quickly found out who the top dog and best instructor in the school was: John Danaher. In fact, John is arguably the best coach in the world and one of the greatest minds in the history of martial arts and certainly modern martial arts.

---

[4] Ep. 4: Rich Byrne | Taking Risks & How to Get It All Done

Making Space

Rich's first lesson with John Danaher wasn't about how to dominate his opponent or beat someone up. John taught Rich one simple concept: how to escape when someone is mounted on top of you.

Newcomers to jiu jitsu wonder why fights often end up on the ground, unlike in boxing, where opponents stand in front of each other and exchange punches. In real-life altercations captured on video, it's not uncommon to see two people throwing a few punches before grappling and rolling around on the ground. That's because when someone tries to punch you, your natural response is to close the distance and hold them tightly to prevent further blows. This instinctive reaction is a survival mechanism that can cause both parties to trip and fall to the ground. Unfortunately, if you're fighting someone who is physically stronger than you, you may find yourself on the bottom, which is a disadvantageous position if you're untrained.

Brazilian jiu jitsu is the art of taking someone to the ground on purpose and being able to control and submit them.

When you're being held down against your will and you're not trained, you can't just get away. And the reverse is true as well. To someone who is trained, holding someone down against their will is easy, and it is virtually impossible to escape. Even people who are highly, highly trained experts can't escape when they face experts who are better than them.

Take Freddy Trillo. Freddy is a Brazilian jiu jitsu

black belt, as well as a thirty-year veteran of the Miami-Dade Police SWAT. Today, he's a full-time Brazilian jiu jitsu instructor who focuses on helping train police officers.

When Freddy started his police career in the early nineties, he was a small, skinny guy. During a routine traffic stop, he asked to see identification from a guy who looked nervous and shaky. The guy handed over the license—which clearly wasn't his. Freddy looked up, and before he knew what was happening, the guy had tackled him to the ground and started beating him senseless.

Recounting the story to me on my podcast, Freddy said, "When you're being beaten within seconds of your life, all the pain goes away. You're in your head, having an out-of-body experience, thinking, *Is this really happening to me?*"[5] It was the same experience I had when I was in the ocean drowning: *I can't believe I'm about to die. I can't believe I'm drowning right now.*

Freddy was lucky: bystanders intervened and pulled the guy off him before he beat Freddy to death. Freddy decided that if he was going to continue his career in law enforcement, he had to learn how to protect himself. That goal sent him down the path of finding Brazilian jiu jitsu, which gave him the incredible superpower of being able to control people twice his size when making arrests.

Whether you're Rich Byrne leading a multibillion-dollar company or Freddy getting beaten almost to

---

[5] Ep. 26: Freddy Trillo | Black Belt Police & SWAT Veteran

death on the street, the principle of how to deal with someone on top of you—whether physically or metaphorically—is an important lesson to learn.

Business Principle: Making Space to Think

In early 2020, I began to hear the rumblings of a new disease they were calling coronavirus, or COVID-19, coming out of China. It quickly spread to Italy, and I remember watching what was happening on the news. It seemed like a movie. Because the situation seemed blown out of proportion and I didn't believe the hysteria, on March 3, I took my infant son down to Florida to celebrate my grandfather's ninety-second birthday. My wife was finishing up her surgical residency at Lenox Hill Hospital in New York, so she wasn't able to come with us.

While we were there, we went out to lunch with my wife's aunt—who wore a mask. I thought, *I cannot believe this woman is wearing a mask to lunch.* I thought she was succumbing to the hysteria. I kept telling myself there was no way this was going to be a big deal. I never could have imagined governments around the world stopping the global economy.

By the time we left Florida, however, I realized the situation was getting serious. The news coming out of Italy was crazy: quarantining, mass death, public panic. Returning to New York, I called an emergency meeting with the entire Mixology staff on Monday morning, March 9. I told them to calm down. We'd been through this situation before with swine flu, Zika, bird flu, SARS, Ebola, etc. I told them that this, too, would pass, and we'd figure it out.

A few short days later, on March 13, 2020, the governor announced that the first cases had hit New York. Then there were five cases. Five turned to ten. Ten turned to a hundred. Then the news was predicting millions of people might die, and in order to stop the spread, we had to quarantine for two weeks. In essence, we had to go into our houses and "hunker down."

So I closed down my office. I packed up everything as if I wasn't coming back. I drove into Manhattan, picked up my wife and son, and packed up our apartment. My wife asked, "What should we take?"

Me: Grab a suitcase, and pack the food.

My wife: The food? What are you talking about?

Me: If they're sending us home, there's a very distinct possibility that things are going to get bad. Very, very bad.

I knew how bad things could get firsthand. In 2012, one of the formative moments of my career was when Hurricane Sandy hit New York City. It was the first time in my life that I saw Manhattan without power for almost a week. Long Island ran out of gas after three days. The stores ran out of food within a few days.

I remember the feeling of carrying food through New York City to my friend's apartment on the Upper East Side because I didn't know when power would be restored to Lower Manhattan. My wife didn't live in New York City during Sandy, so she had no idea how quickly society unraveled.

December 2019: The first cases of COVID-19 are reported in Wuhan, China.

January 2020: The World Health Organization (WHO) is alerted to the outbreak and declares it a global health emergency.

January 23, 2020: China locks down Wuhan, a city of 11 million people, to try and contain the spread of the virus.

February 2020: The virus spreads to Italy, where it quickly becomes a major outbreak.

February 29, 2020: The first case of COVID-19 is reported in New York, a woman who had recently returned from Iran.

March 1, 2020: New York Governor Andrew Cuomo announces the first case of COVID-19 in the state and declares a state of emergency.

March 7, 2020: New York reports its first COVID-19 death.

March 13, 2020: Governor Cuomo announces a state-wide shutdown, closing schools, restaurants, and non-essential businesses.

March 22, 2020: New York reports over 15,000 cases of COVID-19, the most of any state in the US.

April 6, 2020: New York reports its highest single-day death toll from COVID-19 with 731 deaths.

April 10, 2020: Governor Cuomo extends the state-wide shutdown until April 29th.

May 2020: New York begins to see a decline in new cases and deaths from COVID-19.

May 15, 2020: New York begins a phased reopening plan, allowing some businesses to reopen with strict guidelines.

All of these images of Sandy were flashing through my head. My thoughts were filled with ideas of preparedness and preparation. I thought, *We are not prepared for a pandemic. We are not prepared for millions of people to die.* I packed up my family, and when we left the apartment, I looked at my wife and said, "Be prepared to never come back here again. There's likely going to be rioting in the streets and food shortages." She couldn't wrap her head around that.

Thankfully, my parents had a summer home in the Hamptons, and my family; our nanny, Gloria; my brother, Tyler, and his wife, Jessica; my sister, Gabrielle, and her husband (fiancé at the time), Jared; and my cousin Jill all moved into the house together.

I drove back to my office the next day to wrap up everything with my controller (and right-hand man), Eugene Parisi. It's important to know that in the fashion and apparel business, May through December are typically extremely busy months, while the first quarter, January through March, is usually very quiet. In fact, many retail and fashion businesses lose money in the first quarter of the year and run at a planned deficit.

Mixology is no different. We usually carry a deficit at the beginning of the year, and we use our banking relationships to bridge this gap. This means we borrow money on our credit lines to pay for inventory, overhead, and rent. Then, by the end of spring into the start of summer, we start to break even.

Then, through the second half of the year, we begin

to generate profit. That's where the phrase "Black Friday" comes from. Historically, businesses would "go into black" or profit, around Thanksgiving from customers preparing for the holiday season.

So while Mixology was running close to a million-dollar loss going into March 2020, it was a planned loss. We'd budgeted for it. We had a plan—except if you're not allowed to remain in business—if you close the doors and send everybody home—you're losing a million dollars outright.

Standing in the office, I turned to Eugene and said, "Do an analysis for me. How much cash do we have right now?"

At any given time in business, you have money going in—hundreds of thousands of dollars in the case of Mixology—and money going out. You're simultaneously making sales and paying bills. Depending on where you are in the year, sometimes you have millions of dollars of cash in the bank, and sometimes you have tens or hundreds of thousands of dollars in the bank.

On March 17, 2020, after Eugene did his reconciliation and knowing we were losing a million dollars on the books, we had $9,000 in cash. For a company of Mixology's size, $9,000 doesn't even pay one rent check.

I told Eugene to help me call our bankers. "Tap all of our credit lines, and get all the cash we can. We need to build our cash reserves."

I personally called Scott McGrath at BNB Bank (which has since merged with Dime Bank), and said,

"Scott, we need to tap 100 percent of our credit. Will you honor our credit line?"

I knew every one of his clients was calling him at the same time, yet he told me, "We've got your back." We went from $9,000 to $159,000 in cash.

Eugene and I called every bank we had a relationship with, some of which had our back and some of which said they couldn't honor the credit lines. Over the course of the morning, we built our cash position. Our next step was to see who we owed money to that month.

Eugene gave me a list of all of Mixology's landlords, key vendors, and service providers. I called each person, one by one, and told them, "I don't know when this is going to be over. I don't know if I'm going to be able to pay you."

Almost every single one said, "Jordan, this is unprecedented. We're all in this together. We're going to figure it out together." It helped that, up until this point, I had never missed a rent, service, or vendor payment. I knew that it was terrifying for them, too, however. If I didn't pay them, how would they pay their rent, their employees, their overhead?

I promised each of them that I would pay them as soon as I could, but put yourself in that moment. When someone's telling you that they can't pay you, it's not a good feeling. It's a terrible and unsettling feeling— one I had to give to people over and over.

I had to inspire and stay in front of my team to lead. Unfortunately, part of leading included having to furlough some of my team—170 out of 200. There were several people on the team who were so supportive and understanding, including several who volunteered as tribute because their partners had jobs that could support them through this season, including Bryan Sanders, Rebecca Kobetz, and Patricia Papataros.

I hated making these calls. These phone calls are terrifying to make. When you have to sit down and make these calls to tell these people who have been there for you, sometimes for years, "I'm so sorry, but I need to furlough you, and I don't know when I'm going to bring you back," it's scary.

John Danaher and I discussed on the podcast that language is a human superpower. It's incredibly important that you get out in front of all of your stakeholders, community, and employees, all of whom are waiting to hear from you. You need to stand up and let them know what's going on. Once all of my phone calls were made, I created a series of statements that included letters and direct communication to all of my employees and stakeholders detailing the specifics of our current plan. That plan included the Edwards family not taking a single dollar until all of our stakeholders, including every furloughed employee, were repaid.

As hard as it is to make these decisions, you still have to make them fast. I didn't know if they would be the right decisions, and there was no guarantee I would be successful. I did, however, have experience in crises.

Let's flash back to 2012.

Learning from Crisis and Failure

On October 29, 2012, Hurricane Sandy hit New York. The storm was devastating to Long Island, Manhattan, New Jersey, and the southern part of Connecticut. More than ten years later, there are parts of the Manhattan subway system that are still affected by Hurricane Sandy.

The destruction of Hurricane Sandy put Mixology Clothing Company to the absolute test.

Before Sandy hit, Mixology had six stores that ranged from Westport, Connecticut, all the way out to Southampton on the east end of Long Island. After Sandy, Mixology became insolvent. Jon (my former business partner) came back to my dad and said, "Glenn, we need money. We bought about half a million dollars' worth of goods that are incoming, and the business has been shut down for weeks.

In the end, the business was shut down for almost three months because all of our employees' and customers' homes were literally underwater. They lost their cars, their furniture, their clothes, their family pictures—everything.

Before agreeing to another investment, my dad asked me to spend a few days with Jon, review the books and records, and advise him on whether or not to keep the business open. Up until that point, my only involvement in the business was helping create the website with no real operating role other than cheerleader and advisor.

I met with Jon in the back of our Hewlett, New York,

store, and asked to see both the current month- and year-to-date profit and loss statements. Jon replied, "I don't have them."

Me:	Okay. You just spent half a million dollars at that trade show in Las Vegas. Can you show me those receipts?
Jon:	I don't have any.
Me:	(Shocked) How do you know when the goods are going to show up or even what you bought?
Jon:	Well, when they show up, we'll receive them.

It quickly became apparent that Mixology had grown beyond the scope of his small business capabilities. My dad had pushed Jon hard to expand to those six stores. And while there were no official books, I was able to go into the point of sales system to review overall sales to find Mixology had generated over $2 million in 2012. I knew this was a serious business, making serious money. It just didn't have any business controls in place (we'll talk more about control in Chapter 2).

I went back to my dad and said, "If we add the basic controls we have in our real estate business— bookkeeping, POs, invoicing, team meetings once a week—I think we can turn Mixology around pretty quickly."

I joined Mixology Clothing Company with no official role and zero pay. The very first thing I did was institute a Tuesday team meeting. Why Tuesdays? When I was in college, I was president of my fraternity, and I held Monday meetings. Except because most holidays fall on Mondays, we had to keep skipping meetings, so they moved to Tuesdays. I know this seems like a small detail, but it's a great lesson on the small techniques and tactics you begin to use from your collection of life lessons. Plus, I knew retail was all about the weekend sales, so I would need to review books and records on Mondays, leaving Tuesdays as the perfect day for our meetings.

My first Tuesday meeting included myself, my dad, Jon, and Renee, and my first question was directed at Jon: "What do you think we need to do?" He listed four people he thought we needed to fire. Looking back, I understand his panic. He was incredibly stressed and thought he was losing another business.

I immediately said, "We're not firing anyone."

My dad chimed in and said, "The first thing we need to do is close three of our six stores." Jon did not agree.

Jon, nervous and exasperated, said, "If we close down three of our stores, people are going to think we're going out of business."

My dad, ever the sage businessman, said unemotionally, "If you don't close down three stores, you will go out of business. Do you want people to think you're going out of business or actually go out of business?"

We closed down three stores, and then I addressed the suggestion of firing people. One of the people he wanted to terminate was, at that point, one of our longest-serving employees (a consultant), Danielle Stein, who worked for us out in Los Angeles as a buyer.

Instead of firing her, I immediately got on a plane and flew out to LA to meet with her in person. Danielle was a consultant who worked with several other clients as well. Knowing she had a lot of industry knowledge, I asked her, "Danielle, what is Mixology not doing that your other best clients are doing?"

She replied, "You don't give me budgets."

Before she could say another word, I said, "Stop! Who does the budgets?"

Danielle said, "Your inventory planner." (A role that we didn't have.)

I asked for a recommendation, and she immediately connected me with a woman named Margo Kopman. I left that meeting an hour later with a notepad full of good tips and drove across town to the Mondrian Hotel in Santa Monica to meet with Margo. I walked her through our current situation: lots of revenue, hurricane destruction, no POs or bookkeeping, etc. She listened carefully before explaining to me what we needed to do next. At the end of the meeting, I hired her.

I was sitting on my pseudo-cousin Nick Roberts's couch when I called my dad and said, "Dad, I think I'm onto something. Let's keep this business open." I flew back to New York after hiring Margo. I kept Danielle, along with our other longtime employees who had been floated to fire, Randi Spellman and Crystal Cagno. Today, more than ten years later, all those people are still with the company and are some of our key executives.

In the wake of Hurricane Sandy, Margo said something I'll never forget: "Jordan, we're gonna double the size of your business with three fewer stores, and we're gonna buy less inventory doing it."

And we did just that. Six months after Hurricane Sandy, we had doubled the business with three fewer stores on a run rate. About a year after that, my dad made me the president of Mixology, and I started growing the business into the company it is today. Over the next two and half years, I grew the business with a tremendous amount of success. I began to feel invincible.

I decided our next step should be expanding into wholesale manufacturing, so I hired one of our key vendors, along with his two team members, to run our manufacturing and creative process. This experiment turned out to be a complete failure—and an expensive one.

My risk to invest in manufacturing cost Mixology's wholesale business over a million dollars. It was a failed partnership and endeavor that left me with a lot of egg on my face. However, it did teach me a lot about my business, fashion, taking risks, and what does and does not work.

(Pete Roberts, CEO and founder of Origin and Jocko Fuel, called these moments "tuition" on the podcast, and I have been using that term ever since.[6] When you fail and don't quit, it's just tuition.)

---

[6] Ep. 45: Pete Roberts | Origin: Made in America

The biggest lesson I learned was that it was time to move from bookkeepers to a professional accountant and controller. I hired Eugene Parisi (who you'll learn more about in Chapter 2), who, in his first year with Mixology, saved the business a million dollars. He took my million-dollar loss and swung us into a million-dollar profit. And so Mixology continued to grow. We hired better people, opened more stores, and improved every process and division.

When the 2020 pandemic hit, I knew what would happen because it had happened before. There's a quote I love that says, "You don't rise to the level of your expectation. You fall to your level of training."

My training was cut through the recessions, through Hurricane Sandy, through my continuous learning (taking classes and reading books), and by living and making mistakes in previous businesses.

I watched as other entrepreneurs and businesses didn't have the answers to the questions that arose as the world shut down. They were frozen and didn't know what to do. I was able to make these decisions in real-time because of all the years leading up to this moment. That doesn't mean I didn't first experience the feeling of drowning.

My first instinct was to tell my team there was no way this was ever going to happen. Then it happened. I had a moment of thinking, *Oh my g-d, I might die. My company might go out of business. My family's not safe.* Unlike when I was drowning in the ocean, I had twelve years of business experience at that point, having lived through the Great Recession and then

Hurricane Sandy, and having been the leader of a company that had made bad decisions, most notably in my failed manufacturing venture. This time I knew what to do.

That's what business jiu jitsu is: having the training, experience, and confidence to find the answers. Over seven hundred thousand businesses of all sizes, from hundred-year-old institutions and major corporations all the way down to mom-and-pop corner shops, almost immediately went out of business due to the pandemic. Why did some companies do really well, and why did some fail?

It depended on what you were doing before March 17, 2020. How were you training? What were you reading? How were you operating? Think of the story of three little pigs: did you build the straw house, the wood house, or the brick house? Or had you not started building a house at all?

Mat Chat

A common piece of advice for new business owners is to decide what your core values are. Core values are the ideals and principles that (should) influence every decision and action made by the leadership and employees.

Many people pick traits they want to embody (original or cool) or buzzwords (integrity or honesty) without considering why those words are important to them. While it's important to start out with a few chosen values, I've found that your true core values are actually developed and potentially also revealed or uncovered over time as you solve problems.

(And if you don't like what you're finding your values to be? Well, that's a lesson all on its own.)

At Mixology Clothing Company, all of our core values can either be traced back to times when we needed to correct a behavior or are proved so vital that we wanted to make sure everyone knew why we care about that value. For example, one of our core values is that we pay our vendors, landlords, and service providers first.

Your core values, all of them, make up the operating system of how your business is run. If you have great core values that you and your team follow, your business is going to run very, very well.

When COVID hit, I had to make rapid decisions, but I didn't have time to stop and think about my core values. They had to be a part of me, the way that jiu jitsu techniques are a part of me. I had to operate off muscle memory.

Core values won't suddenly appear when everything goes wrong. You're going to operate the same way you have been operating. That's why having a strict set of core values is so important in both life and business: it guides you. You can't remember every email, text, and decision you make. But if you make every decision and action through the lens of your core values, not as words on paper but in lived actions, you're protected.

My core values are one of the reasons that our bankers came through for us. They knew I wasn't a fly-by-night scam artist trying to cut corners. It's also why our service providers extended grace to us, such as Margo Kopman continuing to work with only the promise of future pay. Because of our core value "we pay our landlords, vendors, and service providers first," which means we pay everyone before my family takes a single dollar, when I called Scott McGrath to tap my full credit line, he said yes. If I had been a terrible client who was always late repaying my financial obligations, and he had to choose between their best customer and me, who do you think he would have chosen?

When you live your life by solid core values, you can feel sure you've done everything the right way when shit does hit the fan. Now that's not to say you won't make mistakes. You're not always going to make the right decisions or hold up to your core values. Ultimately, we're human, and humans aren't perfect. However, we can surround ourselves with the right people who will help keep us on the path. Whether it's attorneys, accountants, partners, or friends, you need to ensure the people around you are of high integrity.

For example, my friends Ryann and Scott, a married couple, are of the highest integrity, and they have always ensured I stay true to my integrity as well. Years ago, I had the opportunity to begin a romantic relationship with the ex-girlfriend of one of my best friends. She was beautiful and also one of my best friends. I was lonely, and many of my friends were starting to get married and have children. I was desperate to find someone and ready to make a bad mistake—doing something that had been done to me once before and that had wounded me deeply.

When I told Ryann and Scott I was planning to start this relationship, they were brutally honest with me. They told me the truth, regardless of whether I wanted to hear it, and it became one of the most important moments of my life because a few weeks later, I met my wife. If they hadn't been honest about the mistake I was about to make, my whole life could have had a very different outcome.

Too many entrepreneurs decide they want to save money and surround themselves with "yes men," so they find terrible partners, attorneys, accountants, etc., and then they're surprised when bad things happen.

Because mistakes are one thing, but if you've been involved in sketchy activities, what kind of issues will pop up when you're in trouble and have to reveal your situation to banks and legitimate organizations?

It's especially hard to live this way when you're a small business, living off the company—when the question is, are you going to send your kids to camp or buy inventory?

Often, your employees don't draw these comparisons. They don't realize the company's owner is trying to make these calculations. And many small business owners milk the company dry for personal benefit. They drive a Mercedes, live in a nice house, and send their kids to expensive camps. Except when the money stops coming in, they have to decide if they're going to pay their mortgage or pay their employees.

Those are the core values that lead to you being one of the 700,000 companies that go out of business during a pandemic. How could you not when you're built on a shaky foundation? Without core values, you'll quickly lose control when a situation hits you out of nowhere.

If you're walking down the street and someone tries to rob you, you don't get a choice in the matter. They're exerting their power on you. And you've either been training in jiu jitsu or not training.

If you have been training, the jiu jitsu takes over, and you might be able to take them to the ground and control them. If you haven't been trained, you're probably going to get your ass kicked or worse. When they have the element of surprise, the will, and the intention, something bad is going to happen to you.

In 2020, COVID jumped the world. The businesses that hadn't been metaphorically training disappeared quickly. The businesses that had trained were able to survive or even thrive.

One of the fundamental ways to make space in jiu jitsu is called the knee-to-elbow escape. It follows a specific set of counterintuitive steps. Following these steps allows you to make space for your body to move into a position that gives you an advantage and provides you a measure of control over your aggressor. In essence, you've neutralized your opponent momentarily.

Today, when I do a knee-to-elbow escape, I perform it without thought. I learned the steps and practiced them for years, learning from each mistake, until it became muscle memory. In the same way, I had business muscle memory to pull from thanks to my experience during Hurricane Sandy and the Great Recession, as well as my continued learning. So when COVID hit, my training kicked in, and I knew exactly what to do.

Now that you've made space, it's time to recover your guard.

Chapter 2

Recovering Your Guard

On August 7, 2010, Chael Sonnen stepped into the ring to face Anderson Silva, the reigning middleweight champion. Leading up to the fight, Sonnen made bold claims about how he would defeat Silva, trash-talking the seemingly invincible champion and talking up his own ability.

And at first, it seemed like Sonnen's trash talk would come true. Sonnen dominated the first four rounds by getting Silva on the ground and landing heavy punch after heavy punch. Silva, however, had been fighting for a long time and had gained well-rounded skills through experience. In the fifth and final round, Sonnen appeared to be on the verge of victory when Silva, fighting off his back, wrapped his legs around Sonnen's arm and neck, securing a triangle armbar submission—with less than two minutes remaining. Silva had successfully defended his middleweight title, grabbing victory from the jaws of defeat.

In Chapter 1, you created space by performing a fundamental technique, specifically the knee-to-elbow escape. I also told you about my journey and learnings during Hurricane Sandy and how I knew what to do—creating my emergency action plan for dealing with the early days of COVID. It should have already sunk in: you're in a fight. If you have been training, your muscle memory has taken over, and you've performed the techniques well enough to go from danger into a neutral position.

But what if you're still in the process of forming that muscle memory? What if you're navigating the unknown terrain without gaining the skills you need yet? You've chosen your core values, but perhaps you haven't had the time to solidify a foundation around them.

Don't worry. I've stood where you are now. Being unfamiliar with this knowledge as a beginner is completely natural. This book is my way of guiding you through these decisions. By learning from my experiences, you'll be better equipped to recognize and handle challenges when they arise in your business.

Jiu Jitsu Principle: Return to Neutral

I picked the logo for the *Business Jiu Jitsu* podcast intentionally. It's a circular brush stroke in the shape of an ensō (also known as an ouroboros). This symbol is found all over ancient mythologies as a representation of rebirth. The ensō reminds you that when you get to the end of your journey or when something catastrophic happens to you, the end is not actually the end. Instead, you start back at the beginning.

In jiu jitsu, returning to the beginning means a return to fundamentals. In business, it's your principles and core values. When you've been at your peak and something knocks you down—like a global pandemic or hurricane—you'll find yourself back in the proverbial valley.

While writing this book, I was operating at my peak for almost a year straight: running three companies, making deals, buying and selling buildings, writing leases, hiring people, training jiu jitsu, working toward (and earning) my EMBA, and recording podcasts. Then, I got COVID. I thought, Oh, I'll just be lying in bed at home, so I'll be able to do some work.

But when I looked at my phone, the words twisted. The emails started to pile up. I figured, Fine, I'll watch a movie instead, but I couldn't even focus on the movie. I found myself at the lowest of lows. So I took my vitamins, rested, and did everything I needed to do in order to get back to neutral. My first night back at the dojo after having COVID felt like I had never practiced jiu jitsu before. I couldn't breathe. I couldn't move. My hands were aching and cramping. All of the movements I could do ten days before—that I had taken for granted—were gone. I knew what I was capable of and what I had done many times before, but my body and actions were many steps behind where I needed to be.

In life and in business, you're going to get knocked

on your ass. You have both hands tied behind your back, and you have to figure out a way to come back from it.

A common adage is "fall down seven times, rise eight." The moment of returning to neutral is the special moment of coming back after being knocked down. The moment of rebirth is going from about to lose your fight or about to be out of business and thinking, "No, you didn't get me down." You're not winning yet; you're not back on the offense. But now that the worst has been thrown at you, you have been able to return to a neutral point.

A good metaphor is dieting. You ate healthy for a whole year and lost twenty-five pounds. Then you fell off a little bit. Then you fell off a little bit more. Before you knew it, you were eating out and drinking every night. You have a wedding coming up, so you try on your wedding dress or tuxedo and hope you can zip it, but you realize you can't.

So you make a commitment to yourself: "I'm going to change." You go out for that first run and eat healthy again for a week straight. While you haven't immediately lost the weight you put on, you are back on the road to being in control of your own destiny. This rebirth is the moment of recovering your guard and catching your breath.

This is an important part of the process that rarely gets talked about. We like to look at successful people and believe that they've always been successful: they're always shredded, always happy; they close every deal and never lose money. But the truth is that the people who are experts, are billionaires, and are seemingly perfect have all experienced this bounce-back moment.

We compare their highlight reels to our behind-the-scenes. We watch influencers on social media and see only what they want us to see. That's not reality. You are going to find out just how hard it can be to build a business or get to the next belt. You have to learn how to dig deeper and stop being afraid of hard things.

When I went back to jiu jitsu after having COVID, I had a tremendous amount of fear because I knew I was going to get beat up. It was embarrassing to have people see me fail, especially because they didn't know what had happened to me. They had no idea I had been sick in bed for over a week. They simply knew that two weeks ago I was able to best them easily, and now they could cut through me like warm butter.

This moment of embarrassment is enough to keep most people off the mat and get them to stop returning to training. I understand. Being able to fight through these moments and make a comeback is extremely hard. But the people who compete at the highest levels are those who never give up and are relentless in their efforts to come back.

Each time you fail or face a setback, you learn about how to recover your guard—and, as a result, you get faster at recovering your guard.

In jiu jitsu, you have to build your knowledge up before you can learn how to use speed. And as Sun-Tzu counseled centuries ago, "In a world in which many people are indecisive and overly cautious, the use of speed will bring you untold power."7 The more times you've been through a crisis, the more experience you have, and the less fearful you are of being in dangerous situations. The faster you are at getting back to neutral, the faster you can go on the offense.

Some people on a diet will have one cheat meal, accept it, and get right back to their diet. The same goes with jiu jitsu. You might be consistent for six months and then take a break for a vacation. The faster you can get back on the mat, the faster you can recover. You won't be perfect on the first day or on the second, but the faster you get back to training, the quicker you get back to where you were.

Once you start again, you need to be elastic; if you're too rigid, you'll break. You can't be hard on yourself when you fall off the wagon. Know how to laugh at yourself and think, I've been through this before. I know what to do. This is where muscle memory comes in once again. All the work you've done in the past will help you when you get back on track.

Once you've created space from someone attacking you using the knee-to-elbow escape, for example, you return to guard. Your legs are wrapped around your opponent, either giving you some advantage over them or allowing you to rest a moment in a neutral position and catch your breath.

Neutral guard is your moment to collect yourself, keep your opponent at bay, and, at the very least, stop

---

7 Robert Greene, 33 Strategies of War. New York: Penguin Group, 2006.

them from attacking you. This scenario means someone has attacked you and thrown you to the ground; however, despite their effort, you've been able to recover your guard while they've exerted tremendous energy. The fact that you've been able to get back to a neutral position can be extremely disheartening to them. Think of Rocky versus the Russian Drago in Rocky IV. Drago had thrown everything he had, but Rocky was still moving forward.

As long as you keep showing up every single day and trying to get a little bit better, you're probably going to do well in the long run in both jiu jitsu and business. But what if someone with a ten-year-old business has lost the passion and drive, so they stop showing up and stop learning? Thinking they know everything, they don't read more books, don't go to seminars, and don't talk to mentors. They don't even realize they are in a bad position. This can happen to businesses of any age or size, from brand new to a hundred years old, and is why, as we saw during COVID, businesses you never would have thought could go out of business went out of business.

Business Principle: Controlling Your Processes

Mixology needed to recover our guard on the heels of the government forcing us to shut down. Thankfully, unlike with Hurricane Sandy, we were prepared to act quickly.

On March 17, Governor Cuomo told New York

"nonessential" businesses had to shut down. It was time for Mixology to start making decisions.

Now, if you were a small business going into COVID having made poor decisions—you owed people money, you hadn't built your cash reserves, you didn't have core values in place—you were going to have an exceptionally difficult time surviving. And in fact, those were the first businesses to crumble.

My CFO, Eugene Parisi, joined Mixology in 2015. From 2013–2015, between Mixology and Chart Organization (my real estate investment company), we had twelve different mediocre bookkeepers—it was like a revolving door. Yes, we were a small business, but you still need good financial controls to run a successful business no matter the size. During those three years, we did not have good financial controls.

A few definitions for those who may not have heard these terms before. A controller is the person who oversees a company's accounting operations, including maintaining accounting records, payrolls, and taxes; managing budgets; reconciling accounts; performing audits and financial forecasting; and helping make strategic financial decisions. Financial controls are the procedures and policies that help companies manage their cash flow, create budgets, and protect against potential threats, such as fraud or error.

One of the most common complaints I hear in business, especially on the heels of COVID, is how hard it is to find good people, let alone great people.

You interview someone; you think they're going to be amazing—they say all the right things—and it turns out anything but amazing. This was the case for all the bookkeepers during that period; however, two of these hires stand out for the wrong reasons.

The first bookkeeper proved to be less proficient in the craft than expected. She talked her way into the role due to a need for any job, not understanding how much she needed to know about money and bookkeeping. Bookkeeping is a technical skill that involves a lot more than keeping and filing papers. It only took a few weeks to realize that while she was a very nice person, she did not know how to do the job.

The next person claimed she had been a CFO-level accountant and had included several CFO-level roles on her resume. She seemed highly competent in the interview. I brought her in with very, very high expectations that she was the right person. And it seemed like she was—for a few weeks.

Over time, it became clear that she was making mistakes. Her mood was erratic as well. Some days she came in with very low energy, extremely tired, and moody. Other days she came in excited, peppy, talkative, and happy. It turned out that she was a severe alcoholic. When she was moody, it was because she was hungover. She was barely able to get work done and made lots of mistakes. When she was happy, she was drunk—and also made mistakes. She didn't last long either and cost the company a lot of time and money while she was there.

Sometimes, in order to find the right person, you

have to go through the wrong people. I've experienced this in business as well as in relationships and friendships. This doesn't make either of these women bad people. It just makes them people. We're all totally imperfect in our own ways, and we're all deeply flawed.

The reason I shared these stories is to show how important it is to never give up. As soon as one of these stories happened (and there's a story for every one of the twelve), I was back on the hunt. The hunt may have taken a long time, but it was worth it because it led to Eugene.

Before Eugene, despite (and partly because of) the twelve bookkeepers, we barely had any control over our finances. Yet we kept growing the top-line revenue, opening stores, and hiring people. We were doing better little by little until it reached the point where we knew we needed to aim higher.

Now, when most people make their first major hire or major business investment, they start by looking at their "budget." It never seems like there's enough budget for anything. You think you're not making a lot of money, or you're right at breakeven.

Say you're currently paying your bookkeeper $50,000, and you find that a better bookkeeper or controller will cost $90,000. It's hard to squeeze out that extra $40,000. So where do you get the money?

What I learned was that you don't look at the way the business is currently operating to find the budget. You need to look at the business as it will be once you fix the problems the investment is going to fix. You have to ask yourself, "What problem am I trying to solve? And if I do a good job and invest this money, how much money will it unlock?"

When I realized it was time to level up our bookkeeping, I looked at my profit and loss statement, and I looked at my expenditures. Then, I thought about how much someone truly skilled in finance should be able to save us. I estimated a controller, whose job is to control expenses with good financial processes and procedures, would save us at least $500,000.

I started the process of looking for a controller. In the first interview with Eugene, I told him, "I can't teach you anything about bookkeeping. I can't teach you anything about accounting. You have to know your job, come to this company, and apply your skills and knowledge." I knew that if he were a good fit, he'd be able to come in and turn Mixology's finances around.

I mentioned in the introduction that accounting is the language of business, to build on that I can say Eugene is a master communicator. I hired him thinking he would save us about $500,000, and was shocked when he saved the company $1 million in the first year. He doubled my expectations.

As a CEO or business leader, one of your jobs is to understand how to take a measured risk, make an investment, and then see the investment through. While this can seem as abstract as learning a technique in jiu jitsu, learning how to budget, how to hire, and how to create controls is actually very technical. It's something that you can learn through books, newspapers, articles, trade journals, podcasts, continuing education, YouTube, and now AI.

One of the things I did every day was read *Women's Wear Daily*, a trade journal. Reading it, I started learning about the fashion business through the trials and tribulations of other businesses. Then, as I started reading books about the topics brought up in these articles, I realized that all the answers to my questions existed. I would start to say things to myself like "That is exactly what we're going through," "I know that problem, I fixed that problem already," or "I need to do that!"

Fast forward to March 2020. When the shit hit the fan, Mixology had already had five successful years of prudent financial controls budgeting well, paying every bill, paying every landlord, and paying every vendor. We were like a conditioned athlete heading into the Super Bowl—except we didn't know the Super Bowl was going to happen.

We had to rely on the techniques we had practiced over and over again for years. It's like learning any technique in jiu jitsu. Each time I've learned an armbar, I understand the details a little bit more.

When you're blindsided, you have to fall back on the techniques you've learned over a long period of time in business and fall back on your good habits in order to succeed.

As we discussed in Chapter 1, the first two things I asked Eugene to do were tell me how much cash we had on hand ($9,000) and give me a list of our accounts payable in descending order of who we owed the most money to, how much, and when. He was able to give me both of these things rapidly, within minutes.

This is huge. Many businesses have no handle on their finances on a day-to-day basis. That's because most don't reconcile their sales or invoices daily. Instead, many businesses, especially small ones, wait for their accountant to come to them at the end of the month and tell them if they're making or losing money. They hide from the books. They hide from the expenses. What they don't know terrifies them.

Understanding the intricate balance of your finances is pivotal, transcending beyond merely observing the cash balance in your bank account. This approach might have sufficed for my grandfather sixty years ago, but today's financial landscape, particularly in the United States, demands a more nuanced method known as accrual accounting. This method necessitates recording revenues and expenses at the time they are earned or incurred, not merely when cash changes hands. It's a system that presents a more accurate financial picture by accounting for pending obligations and receivables.

Consider this: your business shows a cash reserve of $100,000. However, under accrual accounting, if $65,000 of that sum represents sales yet to be collected, your immediate cash position is overstated by this amount. It's crucial to understand that while this $65,000 is recognized as revenue, it does not equate to immediate liquidity.

Eugene's daily cash reconciliation practice, while meticulous, is just one piece of the puzzle. It ensures precise tracking of cash transactions but must be complemented with accrual accounting to fully grasp our financial standing. This dual approach allows us to not only track what's in our bank but also to anticipate future cash flows, understanding both our current and forthcoming financial obligations and assets. It's a comprehensive strategy that empowers us to navigate the complexities of financial management effectively.

Having an up-to-the-minute understanding of your actual cash runway is vital. Without that understanding, I would not have been able to have the honest conversations I needed to have to build our cash runway and be proactive in talking with our vendors.

When I had finished following the action plan outlined in Chapter 1, even though I knew I had months of hard work ahead of me, I had gotten in front of it all. I had made an action plan. I had called all of my key vendors. I had spoken to my bankers. I had talked to my landlords.

We barely started the first battle, but I knew I wasn't dead. I knew I was not losing. I had recovered my guard.

Mat Chat

The knee-to-elbow escape is one of the most fundamental techniques you learn in jiu jitsu. It's simple to learn. Once you learn it and start to master it, you can be an absolute novice in almost every other part of jiu jitsu and still make it so no untrained combatants can hold you down. Even an advanced practitioner will have a hard time.

But you have to keep drilling this technique in practice over and over. What you're doing is following a technical learning framework: learn the skill, drill the skill, use the skill in live training, and repeat the process over and over again for years on end.

Once you've done it hundreds of times, even if it's only over the course of six months, it will be ingrained in you as muscle memory. So if someone attacks you, you don't have to think, *Okay, let me do my mount escape.* Instead, you simply do it. You won't find yourself lying on your back, flailing your arms, trying to push the person off you. Instead, you will effortlessly use the technique and immediately go into guard recovery.

It's the same with business fundamentals. When a crisis like COVID hits, muscle memory of good financial controls, how to call your bankers, how to write an action plan, and how to get ahead of the problems kicks in.

Within two hours of Governor Cuomo shutting down "nonessential businesses," I had already made my action plan. I had reconciled our cash. I had called my banks, vendors, service providers, and insurance companies. By the time I went home that day to pack up my family, I had gotten as far ahead of the problem as I could up until that moment.

Six months later (even a full year later), I was having conversations with dozens of my tenants who still had not taken step one. They were paralyzed by fear. They didn't know where their cash was. They owed everyone money. They still hadn't spoken to their insurance company. They didn't know how to file PPP (Payroll Protection Program) loans.

PPP loans were a promise from the government that if you kept people on the payroll but couldn't pay for them, the government would lend you money (up to a certain amount) *and* the loan would be forgivable. For example, if your business was closed for three months and you had $100,000 of overhead payroll but no revenue coming in, they would give you $100,000 so long as you could prove you had been paying these people. And if you could prove you used the money properly when the world turned back on, you could get that loan forgiven. This required a lot of trust.

When the government rolls out a new program like this, they let the banks coordinate the process. Think about how many clients Bank of America or Citibank has. You're just a number on a piece of paper to them. Getting this loan depended on what your banking relationships looked like.

When the requirements to qualify for PPP loans were released, they involved providing a lot of data: tax returns, financial statements, and payroll documents. If you had to call your external accountant, who was at home without access to their computers or server, what do you think they were going to say to you? "Great. My other sixty clients all need the same thing."

Because Eugene reconciled the cash daily, all of our financial information was up to the day. When I pulled a financial statement, it was in shape to be able to give it to an investor or banker. This was a huge business superpower that gave us a competitive advantage. He also got up early every morning to read every document, every news article, every bank release, and every Federal Reserve announcement to ensure he was always up to date on the newest information that could help Mixology Clothing Company and Chart Organization.

Because of his dedication, we were one of the first companies in the country to qualify for and receive a PPP loan. To this day, Eugene gets up early to stay on top of all the financial news. I've had several bankers before, during, and after COVID tell me that he's the best CFO they've ever worked with. It's because he's always training. Think of it as planning to run a marathon. You have to go to the gym every day and follow the training program. You can't show up on marathon day and expect to perform.

I had trained every single day, and I was able to use the principles that I had been studying in jiu jitsu and business to make the correct decisions.

After you recover your guard, you can change your mindset, go on the offense, and make the obstacle become the way—the path to winning.[8]

And you have to ask yourself what you are doing now for the next major problem. There will be another pandemic, war, famine, recession, or crisis. There's always a storm on the horizon, so you need to prepare now.

As I said in Chapter 1, you don't rise to the level of

---

[8] This is a reference to the book The Obstacle Is the Way by Ryan Holiday. I highly suggest every business owner read it.

your expectations, you fall to the level of your training. Where are you going to fall when the shit hits the fan? Will you be able to recover your guard quickly so you can go on the offense before your competitor?

Because going on the offense is the next step.

Chapter 3
Foundations of Offense

When you're attacking, you have a sense of purpose. You're putting the competitor on their heels. You're taking charge of a situation; you're creating opportunities and not waiting for things to come to you. It's extremely hard to go on offense when you feel like every single move that you're making is defensive. It's a feeling of drowning.

In Chapter 1, we discussed the feeling of drowning or being blindsided. You didn't ask for this fight, but you're in one. In Chapter 2, we discussed coming back to a neutral position. This feeling of neutrality should be the deep breath, confidence, and energy you need to start your attack.

In jiu jitsu, you don't say on your first day of training, "I'm going to be a professional fighter within the year." One of my teammates and podcast guests, Randy

Brown, is a UFC fighter.[9] I remember the first day that Randy walked into the dojo as a white belt in jiu jitsu and amateur boxer and said, "I want to be in the UFC."

While he was really good, he didn't go to the UFC the next month. He was better than the average white belt, and he had many athletic gifts, but the guy worked hard to get to the UFC. He started off on the amateur circuit where he was undefeated.

He transitioned to the professional local circuit, where he remained undefeated for many years. Eventually, he earned his opportunity in the UFC by distinguishing himself on the YouTube series "Dana White Looking for a Fight."

Jiu Jitsu Principle: Chaining Your Offense Together

When you show up to your first lesson and you don't know anything about jiu jitsu, you think you're going to be able to recreate the moves you see in movies, TV shows, and UFC fights.

I remember watching the UFC well before starting jiu jitsu, seeing someone use an armbar, and trying to apply it to my brother, Tyler. Of course, it didn't work because I didn't know the correct technique. I hadn't learned the fundamental principles of leverage the armbar relies on, the nuances of how to wedge my legs around him, and how to keep him from moving. All white belts have been there, lying on their back pulling

---

[9] Ep. 2: Randy Brown | From Amateur to Pro UFC Athlete & Investing in Loss

on someone's arms, legs not engaged, using every last bit of strength to try to muscle a tap. It's a frustrating feeling.

Colton Crawford is the lead banjo player for the popular band the Dead South; he is also a Brazilian jiu jitsu brown belt. We had a powerful conversation on the podcast relating BJJ to music.[10] Consider a symphony. While it's technically made up of individual notes, it's the combination that makes it music. In the same vein, while your offense is made up of individual techniques, it's chaining those movements together that creates a successful offense.

As a white belt, you want to go on the attack, but you don't know how. You have to begin by learning fundamental techniques and their underlying principles one by one. This builds your foundation, and as you learn more fundamentals, you increase your knowledge base. You have to keep practicing and training each technique over and over.

When you're learning the techniques and starting to put them together as a white belt, what you're learning is how to tread water—you're learning how not to drown. When you become a blue belt, you practice your attacking techniques on white belts. You start to get a little success on your attack, but it's sloppy. You rarely combine techniques, but slowly you learn that you need to use combinations to open someone up in order to submit them.

---

[10] Ep. 72: Colton Crawford | Harmonizing Success in Music and Martial Arts

Then, as you make the transition from blue belt to purple belt, you start learning how to get your offense going. It's not until you get into the middle to late part of purple belt training you learn how to chain your offense together, meaning you move from one technique to the next to the next with smooth movements. Even when someone has no training, it's hard to use any one technique to subdue them (think of a haymaker one-punch knockout). You need to think, move, and act in combinations.

A successful attack combination might go something like this:

1. You attempt an armbar.

2. They defend.

3. You transition to a triangle.

4. They defend.

5. You again transition to an omoplata (shoulder lock).

6. They cannot defend.

7. You submit them and win the match!

As you move up from purple belt to brown belt, all of these techniques and combinations you've been practicing come together into a beautifully executed end result. However, it takes a long time to get to this level and learn how to get your offense going effectively—it took me twelve years to earn my brown belt. Let's dive into how to work in combinations in business and how Mixology got back on the attack.

Business Principle: Start Generating Revenue

During COVID, Mixology Clothing Company did something remarkable. We were forced to close our stores, and I had to furlough 170 of our 200 employees. It was terrible news during a terrifying time.

The remaining thirty employees—who represented our best retail salespeople, key executives, and e-commerce team members—were all we had to keep the business running. And now, we would have to rely solely on our website, losing our most robust sales channel: brick-and-mortar stores.

In a single day, we pivoted and created an action plan. We would use Slack to communicate with each other remotely, Shopify for our website point-of-sale, ARC (agile retail company) inside of Salesforce as a mobile sales device, and Zoom to meet and speak with each other every day.

Interestingly, I had tried and failed on four prior occasions to launch Slack within Mixology. I always thought it would be a great tool for communication, but I was never able to get our employees on board. It's hard to get retail workers who are on their feet all day to embrace new technology, stop what they are doing, and communicate. They were used to using group text and email.

When you're a leader and ask someone to do something, it rarely happens on the first try. I speak with business owners frequently who come to me frustrated because they are under the assumption that every single person in their company is going to bring the same intensity and love for their business that they have.

Everyone comes to their job with different motivations. Some want career advancements. Some just want a job. Some want to stay active and have fun. In my opinion, Dale Carnegie's *How to Win Friends and Influence People* is the greatest business book ever written. It's essentially a step-by-step guide to how to build empathy and listen to people.[11] If you have a team and find yourself saying, "They're not listening to me. Why don't they respect me? Why don't they do what I say?" then this book is for you.

It's hard to build trust with one person, let alone hundreds. They don't have to listen to every word you say. You're not a king or queen. You're not a dictator. I failed to implement Slack the previous four times because I hadn't developed my empathy and leadership skills yet, so they didn't feel the need to listen to me or trust me.

This time, our backs were against the wall. In *33 Strategies of War* by Robert Greene, he explains that you never want to put your army's back against a body of water—unless you decide you want to put your army's back against a body of water. The reason you don't put your back against water is because it's a zero-sum game. It's life or death, all or none. The reason you do want to put your back against water is

---

[11] Dale Carnegie, *How to Win Friends and Influence People*. New York: Gallery Books, 2022.

because you want your army to fight like there's no other option but to win.

I didn't choose COVID, and COVID forced the team's back against the water. Now decisions and processes that may have taken years, or not happened at all, were happening in hours because everyone was on the same page and resolved to survive—to win. However, don't fall into the trap of believing this new, fast-paced mindset is going to last forever.

As a CEO, it was exciting to see things get done so rapidly; it can quickly become intoxicating. But I also knew it wouldn't always be this easy to get the team on board with change. As the months rolled on, the average employee no longer worked with the same COVID haste. The trick as a leader is to connect with your team and create the same mindset without making it a zero-sum game. Understand there's a difference between your team fighting because they have to and fighting because they listen to and trust you.

Mobile Sales Force

We also launched what we called our mobile sales force. What was the mobile sales force? While a normal sales force sold in physical brick-and-mortar stores, the mobile sales force was selling from their phones and computers while they sat at home.

As we've established, after "nonessential" businesses were shut down, everything came to a halt. We stopped paying rent. We stopped paying vendors. We stopped paying everything except for the absolute critical needs. Our main objective was now to sell enough of the inventory we had in stock to pay each person left on the payroll.

In one of the statements released when we were forced to close our doors, I made a pledge that "I will not take $1 from my company until every single employee, service provider, vendor, and landlord are current." The only money I was going to spend was to pay our people: "Every dollar of revenue we generate will go to keeping our key staff employed."

To pay the staff, every salesperson needed to sell $300 a day, either merchandise or gift cards, to try to build up as much momentum as possible. My dad, the chairman of Mixology, had never spent a single day on our retail sales floor. Yet he was the first person to mobilize and start reaching out to all his business connections, friends, and family. For the first few days of COVID, in the deepest, darkest, scariest days when people were so petrified by fear, they didn't want to support or buy. And my team didn't want to ask *other* people to buy from them.

My dad went on the super offensive and had no fear at all of asking people to buy. What happened? The sales started rolling in. My dad started to accumulate $5, then $10, then $100, and on until he reached over $30,000 worth of gift card sales by himself within three weeks. His entire network came out of the woodwork to support him.

At sixty years old, he became our number-one salesperson. He had no fear, trepidation, or embarrassment about asking people to buy as little as

$200–$300. My dad is incredibly successful. He didn't have to do this for us. This was nowhere close to his responsibility. I didn't ask him to help us. He jumped into action because that was the muscle memory he fell (and continues to fall) back on.

While my dad was getting us our first sales, I was working around the clock to mobilize my team, who was terrified and fearful like most people at that time. I spent all day, every day, on the phone in conversations with my team, landlords, and vendors, doing everything I could to move from neutral to offense with our mobile sales force. Day by day, the sales started rolling in.

Maximizing Our Days

The first action item I implemented was having two team sales calls on Zoom daily: the first at 10:00 a.m. and the second at 3:00 p.m.

During our 10:00 a.m. meeting, we talked about how to stay healthy, how to land a client, and how to sell. I would talk to the team about how to use the technology stack we had assembled from their homes (they knew how to use it from the store but not remotely). And then my dad would come on and tell them a joke and get people laughing.

Each morning, someone was called out as the previous day's hero. Everyone had the same goal to sell $300 a day. Yet someone would pull in a $1,500 sale. Or a $2,000 sale. Someone would sell $100 when they hadn't been able to make a single sale in three weeks no matter how hard they tried. And every single day, we would celebrate every single win as a team. Our mantra became, "We cross the finish line all together or not at all."

We created a sales leaderboard, and at first, it was just my dad on the board. Then, three people were on the board. Then five, then six, and then twenty people made it on the board. "Suddenly," we were generating $10,000 a day. In reality, it wasn't sudden but the result of building momentum and chaining together our attack.

Occasionally, someone would feel like they didn't have it in them that day, and everyone would rush to have their back. There were no individual winners or losers. We empowered each other and helped each other. We reviewed each other's messages to our customers to help tweak marketing copy as the news cycle changed.

In the earliest days, the message was about supporting small businesses and watching out for your friends, family, and neighbors. Then, it evolved into being comfy-cozy at home. The message was constantly changing. As we saw messaging that wasn't working, we adjusted and pivoted. As Bruce Lee advised, we were being "like water," which we could do because we were able to stay in touch with each other all day through Slack and Zoom.

We communicated more from March through June 2020 than in the previous ten years of business. The team was developing relationships and trust like never before. They were spread out all over the New York metro area. People 150 miles away who would otherwise only see each other at the holiday dinner were now face to face on Zoom twice a day and "speaking" all day on Slack.

Because we had an extremely powerful, fully integrated technology stack, we never lost a day of momentum. In literally a single day, the team completely reinvented themselves. Contrast that to Hurricane Sandy, when we were shut down for months. My dad, at sixty years old, showed them how to sell in a totally new way (which, in his words, was really "just the old way with a modern twist"), using best-in-class technology to win. That's business jiu jitsu.

One of the reasons I was able to not only succeed but take advantage of the disaster was a few key decisions I had made years before that let us pivot on a dime. As we learned in the previous chapter, you don't rise to the level of your expectations; you fall to the level of your training.

E-Commerce Lessons

In 2011, two years after we founded Mixology Clothing Company, if you wanted to build a website, you had to custom code it from scratch, hire developers, and either host it on servers that you rented in the cloud (which was a relatively new concept then) or buy physical servers to keep on your property. You had to learn every single aspect of website development.

But then, a small startup company called Shopify launched. Shopify's value proposition was that it templatized website building, meaning all you had to do was pick your favorite template and insert your company's products and identity, and they took care of everything else.

My dad and I, when talking about the high-level strategy for Mixology Clothing Company, would ask ourselves, "How are we going to be in the clothing business and not have a website?" Even back in 2011 having a website seemed logical to us. So when we heard about Shopify, we decided to invest in creating a Mixology website. That website lost money for the first few years, but we kept seeing it grow and seeing the effect it had on in-store sales too.

However, when you invest and lose money, it's scary. You want to stop the bleeding. After all, you could be living off this money. Investing and losing hurts the way tapping in jiu jitsu hurts, getting submitted hurts, and taking falls and impact on the ground hurts. But it's mandatory if you want to win down the road.

Fast forward to March 2020: when we were forced to shut down all of our physical stores, the only place left to sell was online. How many of Mixology's direct competitors—other family-owned retail businesses in the Northeast with ten or more retail stores (of which there were approximately ten total)—had legitimate e-commerce operations? I'm not talking about just a website. I mean a legitimate, e-commerce, omnichannel business strategy.

The answer: zero.

Going into COVID, not a single one of Mixology's direct competitors had a full-scale omni-channel e-commerce operation. Two had e-commerce websites. Another five or so had brochure-style websites that had only the bare minimum company information. The rest had no web business to speak of and barely updated their Google listing business pages (which is free and easy to do).

When Mixology was forced to shut down physical stores, we had a full-scale e-commerce operation with a robust support team, our own distribution center, our own creative team, and our own creative studio. That meant we were able to fundamentally shift our business from 90 percent retail and 10 percent e-commerce to 100 percent e-commerce without having to make a single investment. The metaphorical brick house was built and decorated; we just had to walk in.

Not only were we fully set up, but we had already learned all the hard lessons of how to run a profitable e-commerce business thanks to many years of making white belt mistakes and losing money. When the big bad wolf came knocking, we didn't have to build our brick house. It was already built to withstand all the blowing he could do.

Failing to Succeed

The second important decision we had already made was in 2015.

While optimizing our e-commerce site, I noticed we needed more data and tools around our customers. I didn't actually know much about our current customers, and I felt in my gut that I needed great technology to get the data to truly understand our customers' behaviors.

I looked to the market and found Salesforce. Salesforce was the best-in-class CRM (customer relationship management) tool that all the best companies in the world were using. I decided to try to bring Salesforce into the company. It would give my front-line sellers a clienteling tool and a way to keep in touch with customers. And the robust reporting would give me, as the CEO, visibility into the specifics of my customers, including where they lived, how much they spent, what they purchased, and more.

At the time, I was essentially operating two businesses: the stores and the website. They didn't speak to each other well, with the exception of a small app (software application) that fed basic sales information back and forth. Most of the data was siloed, meaning it wasn't shared between operating systems, which is a very common issue even to this day.

I wanted to ensure that if someone shopped on the website and then later that day or the next shopped in a physical store, the team not only had a record of all their purchases (whether online or in-store), but they were also notified of the repeat purchases. After all, someone spending multiple times with us in quick succession in multiple places is a key indicator of a great customer. It should set off every alarm bell.

In short, I wanted a single source of truth for every customer's behavior. But in 2017 when I started working on this problem, no out-of-the-box solution existed. Even in 2024, it's still a problem many companies are trying to solve.

However, I had (and still have) an older POS system called RunIt. RunIt is a legacy system that's an incredibly robust tool fantastic for running a profitable in-store business, except it doesn't have any e-commerce capabilities or open APIs. In order for these systems to talk to each other, I had to build what's called a custom API integration.

API stands for application programming interface, and it's basically the way two pieces of software talk to each other. This is where the term "tech stack" comes in. API lets you stack, or integrate, your systems together. When they're not stacked and "speaking" to each other, they're considered siloed.

New software is built with open APIs. When you download apps on your iPhone that connect to each other and share data, they're built on API frameworks. This is also how Shopify worked, so I figured, how difficult could it be to integrate Shopify, Salesforce, and RunIt?

To integrate all these technologies, I hired a third-party company recommended by Salesforce to build the custom API. They told me it would take six weeks and cost $30,000; I signed on the dotted line. At the end of the six weeks, we didn't have a working API. I was very, very frustrated—and having flashbacks to my disastrous failed wholesale business/partnership—but I stuck with them for another few months. Six weeks turned into six months, and $30,000 turned into $50,000, and I still didn't have a working API. It was time to terminate their contract for nonperformance.

I found and hired a new company, also recommended by Salesforce, to integrate Salesforce with RunIt. Their projected timeline of six weeks turned into six months and then into a year. At this point, I was approaching $200,000 of developer time with this company, and I still didn't have a working integration.

I was now approaching a $250,000 investment into this technology without a working product on the heels of a failed wholesale business and a million-dollar haircut. To say that I was up at night thinking I was a complete failure for losing my company's money and that I was a terrible businessperson would be an understatement. I was beating myself up constantly. I was scared. I was nervous. I thought I was making a costly, massive mistake all over again. However, my wife Danielle often tells me, "When you're ready to give up, you're only two millimeters away from success."

So I went to two members of my team, Anna Katz (now a former team member) and Liz Cioffi, and said, "We're going to terminate this contract. I'm thinking about pulling the plug on this whole project, but before I do, can you two see if you can find one more company?" Anna ripped into our Salesforce account executive, and together, they found a gentleman named Arya Sajedi, the man who saved the project.

When I met with Arya, I gave him an update on everything that had happened so far. Then I asked him, "How long is this going to take you, and how much budget do you need?" He replied with something that was so profound that I've repeated it hundreds of times.

Arya said, "Jordan, you've already had two companies that failed with that approach. I can't give you an exact budget. And I can't tell you how long it's going to take. Why don't you engage me for one month? Let me look under the hood of all your systems. Let me interview your employees. Let me take a look at the software. And then let me give you a recommendation."

At the end of the month, he came back with his findings. He explained, "Both of the companies built very competent technology. It's not that they didn't do a good job at building an API. What they missed was taking the time to actually understand the business. They didn't take the time to understand the other system, RunIt, or learn enough about the fashion retail business. You're actually not that far away from where you want to be." (Thank you, Danielle!)

Then he gave me a very reasonable number and timeline. He said he was confident he could get the API up and running in six weeks—and he did. ARC (Agile Retail Company), which is what we ultimately named the application/API, launched in January 2019. If you're counting, that's three years from when I first purchased Salesforce.

ARC is a system for understanding customer behavior and then being able to reach out to customers via text, email, phone, or direct message. It allows you to see all their purchase histories, which store locations they shopped at, what products they bought, and what sizes they bought. In the industry, this has become known as a "single source of truth" for customer data or the 360-degree view of the customer. ARC has evolved into so much more, and we now run many of our cutting-edge business strategies and tactics on Salesforce using the software.

From January 2019 to June 2019, we ran one marketing campaign. That single campaign generated $500,000 in six months, far exceeding the $350,000 that I had invested over the three-year period. The whole investment had been validated.

ARC is what we used every single day during COVID to be effective working from home because we built it, trained on it, practiced with it, and used it every day leading up to COVID.

The fact that Mixology's entire technology stack was harmonized and able to talk to each other when the storm hit is why we were effectively able to go on the offense and start serving our customers. If you didn't have Shopify, if you didn't have a clienteling tool, if you didn't have all your inventory and customer data, how were you going to be prepared to go on the attack?

Mat Chat

You may be saying, "Jordan, I'm not doing these things right now. What if something happens tomorrow?" My answer: start today.

You need to start creating these habits and making these investments today. The longer you wait, the less time you have to train for the wolf.

For example, say you own a retail clothing business, and you haven't launched on Shopify, and you don't have an omnichannel strategy. You're late to the party. Today's the day to start. If you have a restaurant and you're not on OpenTable or Uber Eats, today's the day to sign up.

You haven't started learning jiu jitsu? Today's the day to start training. There's an adage that says the best time to plant a tree is twenty years ago; the second best time is today. I was able to launch Zoom and Slack rapidly because I invested and struggled for years to launch and master Shopify and Salesforce.

Often people think you start a business and that's it: you own a business and do the thing you love. "I've always wanted to be a jiu jitsu instructor full time." Guess what. It's not just doing jiu jitsu all day. You have to market your business. You have to pay rent. You have to run events. You have to do birthday "classes." You have to teach the kids' class. All of these things are outside the spectrum of what you thought you were going to get to do.

"I want to be a fashion buyer." Because you like shopping? Being in the fashion business is about managing people, running events, shipping and receiving, and handling purchase orders. I don't know anyone who has said, "I want to go into fashion to become a logistics expert." The average person who loves dressing and fashion doesn't realize the extent of the back end of a fashion business. The same goes for a jiu jitsu academy, a team, a company, or any organization.

Being able to attack is not about learning the one knockout punch, fancy kick, or slick technique. Going on the attack is about falling back on all your training.

It's using all the things you've learned up to that point.

An important aspect of going on the attack, however, is knowing how long to attack for. When you go on the offense, you can't keep it up at 100 percent full steam for the entire fight. To stay in the fight, sometimes you simply need to survive the round. To stay in business, sometimes you simply need to survive the day. Understanding how to throttle our attack was the next lesson the Mixology Clothing team had to learn.

Chapter 4
Throttling Your Attack

In the year 279 BC, King Pyrrhus of Epirus engaged the Roman army in a pivotal clash known as the Battle of Asculum.

This encounter marked the second engagement of the Pyrrhic War, a conflict spanning from 280 to 275 BC. The origins and motivations behind this war vary across historical accounts, but a common thread emerges: several Greek cities in southern Italy implored Pyrrhus, who ruled over Epirus along the African coast, to lead their forces against Rome. Fueled by his reputation as a brilliant tactician and swayed by generous gifts, Pyrrhus accepted the request and led the war against Rome.

The battle itself inflicted significant casualties upon both armies. While the Roman forces suffered double the losses incurred by Pyrrhus's troops, the Romans possessed the advantage of swift replenishment, whereas Pyrrhus lacked reinforcements. In a pivotal letter sent to Plutarch, Pyrrhus reportedly wrote, "If we are victorious in one more battle with the

Romans, we shall be utterly ruined." This momentous victory had set him on a path to losing the overarching war.

The term "Pyrrhic victory" emerged from this context, giving rise to the familiar adage "You've won the battle but lost the war." The lesson inherent in the Pyrrhic victory is that a battle is not a solitary event; it's part of a broader war. A strategic commander might face successive defeats in individual battles yet retain an upper hand in the larger conflict thanks to superior forces, deeper insight, and more profound experience. What seems like a series of losses can actually reflect the strength of patience and long-term strategy.

When facing a significant disadvantage, trying to engage in direct competition using the enemy's methods isn't a smart strategy. Trying to replicate their approach or play by their rules is a quick path to failure.

If I'm in direct rivalry with a major competitor many times my size—Nordstrom, for example—trying to outspend them or outmarket them is impractical. I'll never be able to surpass them in marketing or resources, so a different approach is imperative. Otherwise, I'll end up like King Pyrrhus: I may achieve a single victory, but I will always lose the war.

The key to triumph is to choose a strategy that doesn't follow your competition's tactics and mindset. As Sam Walton, founder of Walmart, said, "Don't play your enemy's game—play your own on your own timeline."

Jiu Jitsu Principle: Throttling

If you throw yourself into a match at one hundred miles an hour, "balls to the wall," using 100 percent exertion, you'll experience the real-life version of your energy bar dropping to zero in a video game. It's like burning all your fuel on the first lap of a car race when you still have five hundred laps to go.

An essential part of jiu jitsu is knowing how and when to use energy. Beginners always have to learn this the hard way. No matter how fit they are, no matter how great of an athlete, how many miles they can run or bike, or if they're a literal Olympian, when they train in jiu jitsu for the first time, they experience the same story. Within a few minutes of their first match, they are spent.

Why? Extreme fatigue. Their hands cramp. Their legs cramp. They can't breathe. It feels like drowning. Every muscle in the body clenches because they're using extreme energy in an attempt to win. Experienced practitioners know that you don't want to clench your muscles the entire match.

They also know that there is a time to go fast and a time to go slow, a time to go hard and a time to go soft. Sometimes you want to be rigid; sometimes you want to be loose. Sometimes you should attack, and sometimes you should defend. This is called throttling.

The artful modulation of intensity and pace, throttling is a skill that demands prolonged commitment and discipline to master. Many practitioners won't truly grasp this concept until they earn their purple belts. Similarly, numerous business owners only come to recognize its value after facing setbacks. Embracing this principle becomes indispensable during crises: when blindsided by unforeseen challenges, your clarity might waver, resulting in you defaulting to your ingrained habits and training. In such time, the ability to throttle ensures a considered response, guided by muscle memory and informed by experience.

It's also important to maintain fluidity. My sensei often likens our approach to that of bamboo versus hardwood. While hardwood might seem strong, its rigidity makes it susceptible to breaking in strong winds. Bamboo, on the other hand, possesses a unique blend of strength and flexibility, allowing it to bend without breaking.

While training with our sparring partners, we're encouraged to be like bamboo, embodying fluidity and ease. Adaptability is key; just as bamboo sways with the wind, we must move and adjust to our opponent's actions. Being excessively rigid, like hardwood, not only saps one's energy but also risks compromising resilience. By being relaxed, engaging playfully, and moving fluidly, we position ourselves to harmonize with unfolding situations, allowing us to easily navigate challenges.

In the midst of a grappling match, after expending considerable energy, it's essential to throttle. You must skillfully create space, reestablish your guard, and take a few breaths to rejuvenate and recenter. Only once you're reenergized can you reengage with a strong offense. Masterfully moving between offense and defense, maintaining constant pressure on your adversary while preserving your own energy reserves, is the true art of jiu jitsu.

Business Principle: Don't Hide Behind Busywork

The same idea applies to business. You can keep yourself busy with work morning, noon, and night—24/7/365. But that's not going to keep you in business.

My dad taught me early in my career that sales drive the business, not operations. Yes, operations are extremely important. However, you can have the best operations, the best processes, and the best controls, but without sales, you aren't going anywhere. Sales are the gasoline that keeps your metaphorical car in the race.

When I was in college, I decided I was going to start a T-shirt business. At that time, around 2005, you couldn't simply create a drop-shipping business through Shopify. If you wanted to manufacture clothing at scale (meaning anything over about twenty-five units), you had to go to China.

My dad introduced me to one of his contacts, a man who developed clothing for several big-box retailers, who told me exactly what I needed to do to get my business started. I said, "Great!" And then I went ahead, following all the "rules" I was learning in my undergraduate business program: I made a business plan. I started researching. I looked into insurance. I figured out how to open a bank account. I made a list of everything I needed to figure out. What designs would I be making? How many would I buy of each design? What customers did I want to target?

Weeks turned into months without a single shirt made. After six months, my dad called me to check how the business was going. I told him all about how hard I was working: "I have this business plan I want to show you. I've been meeting with bankers. I have a quote from this insurance company." I was so excited to tell him how I was keeping myself busy. Finally, he interrupted.

"Jordan, stop it. Business is simple: make the T-shirt, sell the T-shirt. Everything else will follow after. **Make the T-shirt. Sell the T-shirt.**"

Of course, I was young, so I thought I knew everything. I told him every reason he was wrong. I told him what they were teaching me in my entrepreneurship program at school. In the end, my dad was 100 percent right. I never took the steps he told me: make and sell the shirts. I wasted a lot of time—and never made a single sale.

Let's return to 2020 and the pandemic. I've often been asked how I knew what to do to keep the business alive. The answer, as you've hopefully learned by now, is that I had been here before. I had learned from mistakes in the past—businesses that failed, businesses that never even got off the ground—and I was incorporating those learnings into my actions.

As the pandemic's initial shocks began to wane, Mixology Clothing Company regained its footing. We started to accept that living out of our homes was the new normal. Yet amid the confines, we saw a broader picture. We weren't alone; the world was in this together, a fact that was overwhelming, humbling, and uniting. And sales began ticking upward.

There's something about even a smidgen of success—it fuels hope. As the team began to see results, there was a subtle shift in our mindset, a growing thought: *Maybe we can win.* But as days became weeks and weeks morphed into months, the initial optimism was tested. This is where the principle of throttling came into play.

It's unrealistic to expect to be "on" constantly, especially during something as demanding as a global pandemic. Adapting was vital. With the team now working remotely, thanks to our trusty mobile Salesforce powered by ARC, the classic "9-to-5" felt archaic. I set a target: $300 per person, per day. While it might seem like a modest goal compared to our usual metrics, during COVID, it felt like scaling a mountain.

Our outreach became intensely personal. Every day involved calls to our friends, family, and loyal customers. Each of them, just like us, was grappling with the pandemic's realities. Early on, our messaging was simple and heartfelt: "Support small businesses," and "Your patronage keeps our company alive." As I declared in Chapter 1, my commitment was unwavering—I wouldn't earn a penny until our full team was back on deck and all of our stakeholders paid in full. Our immediate aim? Generate enough to ensure our team had food on their tables.

Working from the confines of home brought challenges and distractions. Anxiety was palpable. Bleak predictions in the news painted a grim picture—three million lives could be lost in the US alone. The very act of stepping outside to grab essentials like toilet paper felt terrifying as it carried with it the fear of endangering our loved ones.

This weight, this immense responsibility, was something every member of my team felt daily. Some days were good—maybe they made two or three sales. But the next morning, the reset button was hit. It was uncannily like living out *Groundhog Day*—the same walls, the same sweatpants, and the same quest for that elusive quiet corner away from familial chaos.

The big question loomed: how did we find our groove in this chaos? How did we create flow? What would it take to maintain momentum or even a semblance of it? Our daily Zoom morning calls became invaluable. They weren't just about work; they touched upon global updates, government guidelines, and valuable input from our legal and medical allies. I wanted the team to find assurance in our collective decision-making. As I often reiterated, "We can't control what's going to happen tomorrow, and we can't control what happened yesterday, but we can control what we do today."

On our calls, we also discussed what our day should look like. You couldn't wake up in the morning and start emailing and texting customers because most people shop when they're lying in bed at night. I encouraged our team *not* to work in the morning; instead, after our morning Zoom call, they should go for a walk, exercise, eat a healthy breakfast, and spend time with their family. Then, as the day shifted into afternoon, they would start to prepare for selling, including creating a list of who they would reach out to that day so they weren't reaching out to the same ten customers (and eventually annoying them).

The next step was to craft the messaging they would use that day. As the pandemic wore on, we moved from supporting a small business to focusing on comfortable outfits to wear at home while working or watching Netflix. On our afternoon call, we set our sales tactic for the evening.

The most common tactic we used was a social media blitz. This was where every single person in the company, at the same time, showered every single channel—TikTok, Facebook, Instagram, along with email and texting—with the same message (to be clear, the wording was not identical but the core of the message was the same). From 7:00 p.m. to 8:00 p.m., we jointly performed our blitz. And every night around the same time, the sales started rolling in. By 10:00 p.m., we knew if we hit our goal or not. Almost every single day we utilized this strategy we hit our sales goal.

The next day, we followed the same schedule all over again. However, every day there was a different hero. Each day we celebrated the employee with the biggest sales number the night before. This meant that someone from the executive team needed to get up very early in the morning to reconcile the numbers from the night before—usually my sister, Gabby. Gabby went through every single sale, compiled the numbers, and created a leaderboard inside Salesforce that we brought up on our morning call in order to celebrate the hero of the day.

This daily cadence was how we were able to throttle. Compare this to the first few days of COVID when the team was sending out emails for eight hours a day without making a single sale. The new goal was to perform prep work at set times instead of aimlessly working all day, keeping busy but not getting any results. By performing our prep work in the afternoon (throttling into defense), we could go hard and fast during the blitz (throttling into offense). Now the team was spending less time working but making more sales with better mental health (as good as anyone's mental health could be during a global pandemic).

Knowing how to throttle is understanding the difference between what is busywork and what is important, thought-provoking work that's going to generate sales and grow your business. There are many cases of businesses that have earned billions of dollars in revenue but weren't profitable and went bankrupt or out of business (Barneys, Sears, and WeWork, for example). Understanding when you're performing efficient work versus when you're making busywork for yourself is a harsh wakeup call but a critical one.

Tips to Gain Momentum

If you find yourself struggling to kick-start your productivity or feeling swamped to the point of indecision, I'll offer you the same advice my dad often shared with me: start by tackling the simplest tasks first.

Picture yourself lying in bed in the morning, consumed by apprehension over everything waiting for you at work. This is bound to create a sense of overwhelm. I've fallen into this mental trap myself, overthinking the sheer magnitude of managing a team and juggling multiple projects for multiple companies.

To avoid spiraling, I follow my dad's advice, and it starts with keeping a well-structured to-do list. I start every workday by addressing the tiniest, least complicated items first. Frequently, these are the tasks that linger on your list for days, weeks, or even months. They're also the ones that, once you address them, you realize only take a few minutes each to accomplish.

It also helps to gamify your momentum. I've created a game I affectionately call "How Much Can I Get Done Before." Let's say I have a meeting in thirty minutes. Rather than aimlessly browsing social media or perusing emails, I turn to my list and try to check off as many items as possible before the meeting starts. It never ceases to amaze me how many tasks I can accomplish in such a short amount of time.

Even better, this practice always gives me a jolt of momentum and helps me get into a flow state. Think of this approach through the lens of embarking on a run. You wouldn't dash out your front door and launch into an all-out sprint. Instead, you'd start by stretching your muscles, followed by a few minutes of walking, a light jog, and then a full-fledged run. By setting the stage with simple, manageable tasks—akin to warming up your muscles—you create the momentum that helps you tackle the more substantial tasks.

Mat Chat

You must learn how to throttle. You need to know when to turn working hard on and off, when to sell, and when to prepare. In *The 7 Habits of Highly Effective People* by Stephen Covey, there's a principle described as sharpening your saw.[12] Covey tells a fable that I'm paraphrasing here.

An old man comes across a young man in the woods who is trying to cut down a tree. The young man is exasperated, sweating, and frustrated. Clearly, he's been at this for hours. The old man stops him and says, "What are you doing?"

"Can't you see? I'm trying to cut down this tree," replies the young man.

"Did you stop to think you should sharpen your saw?" says the old man.

"I don't have time to sharpen my saw! I have to cut down this tree," the young man cries back desperately.

The lesson of the story is that if the young man had

---

[12] Stephen R. Covey, The 7 Habits of Highly Effective People: Restoring the Character Ethic. New York: Free Press, 2004.

taken the time to prepare and sharpen his saw, he could have cut down the tree faster. Preparing to win is an important aspect of throttling your attack.

One of the ideas I repeated to my team often on our morning Zoom calls was that Mixology was not about individual efforts. We were going to win or lose as a team. We would have to carry each other through the hard days. One employee might have a great sales day while another would call me in tears from fear and overwhelm. The next week, those two employees would switch places, with one killing it and the other breaking down.

As a leader, I had to ensure no fingers were pointing at each other for not performing on a daily basis and there was no claiming one person deserved more pay than another because they had a better week or two. I had to keep military discipline of "we're all in this together." We needed to cross the finish line together because it was the only way to win. After all, if my strongest people ate and killed my weakest people, what would happen when it was time to reopen the stores? I had to think three, four, five months ahead.

Not everyone on your team can be a Tom Brady. You still need the towel boy and the equipment manager and the line painter. The better you can make your best players understand and embody this philosophy, the more successful your company will be as you grow. Your job as a leader is to ensure all your people get along, meet them where they are, and ensure they all feel welcome in your company. This is as much a part of throttling as preparing for hard work and performing hard work.

Walter Isaacson once asked Steve Jobs what he thought his most important creation was, assuming he would say the iPod or Macintosh. "Instead he said it was Apple the company. Making an enduring company, he said, was both far harder and more important than making a great product."[13]

If you don't know how to throttle, your natural instincts are going to be to push people so hard that you break them because of your own stress and desire to win. One of my throttling strategies at my companies is to embrace the fact that there will be ebb and flow in both the business itself and in the employees' lives. There will be a death in the family. Someone will have surgery. Someone will get married and go on their honeymoon. These ebbs and flows are not something the team should feel guilty about.

Don't win the round at the expense of losing the fight. Don't win the day at the expense of losing the month.

---

[13] Walter Isaacson, "The Real Leadership Lessons of Steve Jobs," Harvard Business Review Magazine, April 2012, https://hbr.org/2012/04/the-real-leadership-lessons-of-steve-jobs.

Part Two

Chapter 5
Fear and Failure

When you decide to become an entrepreneur and start a business, it's your job to navigate whatever challenges get thrown at you. It's a dark, scary, and lonely road. People who are constantly paralyzed by fear and can't make decisions fail. According to the U.S. Bureau of Labor Statistics, 20 percent of new businesses fail during the first two years of being open, 45 percent during the first five years, and 65 percent during the first ten years.[14]

I'm not saying you won't feel fear or fail at some point. It's guaranteed that you're going to be fearful and you're going to experience failure. It's how you master these that ultimately decides how successful you are going to be. Even the biggest names such as

---

[14] "Establishment Age and Survival Data," U.S. Bureau of Labor Statistics, October 26, 2022, https://www.bls.gov/bdm/bdmage.htm#:~:text=by%20establishment%20age-,Table%207.%20Survival%20of%20private%20sector%20establishments%20by%20opening%20year.

Jeff Bezos and Elon Musk have experienced fear and failure. In the biography *Elon Musk*, Walter Isaacson reports that Elon would become so stressed about the future of his company that he would be up all night, unable to sleep, vomiting, and experiencing tremendous back pain.[15] No one is immune.

However, you can't let the fear of failure stop you from even starting. If you never step foot in the ocean, you'll never experience the incredible feeling of gliding through the water on a surfboard. It's very hard to take that first step and dive in. The water might be bitter cold. There may be an undertow. You may have never felt the feeling of being totally helpless.

But people who learn to surf also learn to work with these elements. They learn how to dance with, play with, and respect the ocean—while knowing they can never master it. Even the best surfer in the world can't master the waves. Anyone can, however, learn to master their fear of the elements.

Jiu Jitsu Principle: Overcoming Fear

In my experiences as an entrepreneur and jiu jitsu athlete, there are three common ways fear can show up and hold you back: fear of starting, fear of continuing, and fear of finishing.[16] You have to overcome all three of these fears in order to be

---

[15] Walter Isaacson, *Elon Musk*. New York: Simon & Schuster, 2023.

[16] Note: These are not the only three types of fear. These are simply the three types I'm exploring in this book.

successful in jiu jitsu, business, and life.

Fear of Starting

Your mind can come up with hundreds of reasons not to start something like jiu jitsu: "It's dangerous." "It takes up a lot of time." "I don't have time for this." Fear is something that crawls into the back of your mind and can keep you from starting.

One of the most common reasons is fear of failure. You know you're not going to do well or not be good at something. You start telling yourself limiting beliefs: "I'm not in shape." "I'm not fast enough." "I'm not strong enough." "I'm too small."

Then you try to come up with actions you need to take before you can start: "I can't go surfing because I don't have a surfboard." "I need to buy a new wetsuit first." "I need to book private lessons."

All of these excuses are born of the fear of starting. In my first book, *This Is It*, the first chapter is titled "Just Start" because it's the most important action for getting over fear. When I started the business jiu jitsu project, I knew I wanted the end result to be a book (the one you're reading right now, in fact). To write the book, I wanted to perform my own research, which I decided would take the form of a podcast. And because of my many years of jiu jitsu training, years in business, and years of reading, I knew that I needed to simply start.

I had never recorded a podcast before, so I didn't know what I was doing. I didn't have any equipment. However, I was not going to use any of that as an excuse to wait. The same week I decided to start a podcast, I found a nearby recording studio, booked time, and recorded my first episode. Taking action put momentum on my side. Starting, the hardest part, was over.

I learned from my failed T-shirt business, where I failed to overcome the fear of executing my ideas by simply selling. My dad told me to make the shirt and sell the shirt, and I didn't. This time, when I had the idea for the podcast, I recorded the podcast, posted the podcast, and marketed the podcast.

The idea of starting is simple, but it's hard for many people to do. Often, when training in the dojo, opponents stand in front of each other and wait for the other person to do something. They're hesitating.

In 2019, Orlando Sanchez, a black belt ADCC champion, faced Nick Rodriguez, who was only a blue belt. Orlando thought he was going to destroy Nicky Rod easily. They faced each other in the ring and, as soon as the match started, Nicky grabbed Orlando, a beast of a man, pulled behind his head, and threw him to the mat. The fight went on, but from that moment, Nicky Rod had the upper hand and eventually won.

Even though Nicky was technically less superior, he took immediate action and asserted his dominance. In later interviews, Orlando said that whoever takes the initiative first is going to win, which is exactly what Nicky did. The lesson here is clear: when at a severe disadvantage, seize the initiative—boldly overcoming the fear of failure can yield tremendous benefits.

Fear of Continuing

Congratulations! You've beat your fear of starting. You started learning jiu jitsu and have been training for several years, received your white belt, and earned all four stripes on that belt. Now you're about to take the magical step of earning your blue belt. Having a blue belt is like having a superpower, as UFC fighter Luke Cuomo told me years ago.

Transitioning from white belt to blue belt gives you the feeling of satisfaction and accomplishment, which is fantastic—except those feelings can quench your thirst enough to make you feel a little bored because you think you know what you're doing. (In reality, you're only at the beginning.)

My wife, Danielle, gives everyone the advice, "Don't tell anyone that you're going to do something." Don't say you're going on a diet or that you're going to get something. Her reason is simple: the act of saying it is as gratifying as actually doing it. Instead, she says, "Talk about it after it's done. Don't tell me you want to go for a run. Go for the run, and then tell me how it was." I love this advice.

Garry Tonon, a student under John Danehar and an incredible jiu jitsu and mixed martial arts fighter, talked about this concept on his Instagram account and sums it up well:

> The scientific data tells us that if we inform people around us that, for instance, we are going to write a book or that we're going to start a podcast or that we are

going to run a marathon or whatever it happens to be, more often than not, we get feedback that is generally positive in form. I think that's good and to be expected, frankly. If a friend tells us, "Hey, I'm going to write a book" or "I'm going to pursue a new fitness goal" or "I'm going to learn a language," we say, "Great, go for it. You can totally do it. You're very likely to succeed. Go for it. How do you want me to support you? Is there anything I can do to support you?" Those are all, frankly, healthy exchanges. And yet, the data tell us that the positive feedback that we get from others when we announce that we're going after a goal, activate certain reward systems and motivation systems within our brain that then quickly dissipate and then diminish the probability that we'll engage in the type of behaviors that actually lead us to achieve that goal.[17]

This advice is great for jiu jitsu. The ultimate goal is to improve yourself and constantly keep learning the art. Unfortunately, many people stop pursuing this goal after they reach blue belt status. I should know—I was one of them.

When I earned my blue belt, I had a lot going on in

---

[17] Garry Lee Tonon (@garrytonon), "I Can't Speak to the Science of This...," Instagram, video, September 3, 2023, https://www.instagram.com/reel/Cwt5ju-AZUR/.

my life. I was in my late twenties, building my career, and having problems with my ex-girlfriend. I wasn't happy. I wasn't where I wanted to be. I skipped one day. One day's not a big deal, right?

One day turned into a week. A week turned into two. Before I knew it, I hadn't been to jiu jitsu in six weeks. I'll be forever grateful to Matt Culley, one of my professors, friends, and podcast guests, who called me and said, "Hey, I haven't seen you at the dojo in a while. I know it can be a lot to get back in the habit. If you don't want to train with everyone right away, why don't we just meet up and train by ourselves first? Then I can help you get back into the dojo."[18]

Why was this offer so critical? The first time this happened to me, I didn't understand what my problem was. Why couldn't I make myself go back? After many years, and two more lapses, I finally understood. I was scared.

When you miss class, your friends, teammates, and opponents are training. Every day they're getting a little bit better. And if you're not training, you're getting a little bit worse. Whether you know it consciously or subconsciously, you know that you haven't been putting in the work. As my sensei likes to say, "Jiu jitsu is a jealous mistress." If you don't show up, it does not stay put.

Consider the average person who has been training diligently every single day. If they miss one week of jiu

---

[18] Ep. 70: Matt Culley | Entrepreneurial Journey: From Bar Owner to BJJ Master

jitsu because they're on vacation or pull a muscle, it can set them back months. Yes, really.

When this happens, you know that the first day back is going to be painful. Deciding to get up, get dressed, and walk into that dojo is one of the scariest Mondays of your life. I've been there hundreds of times over the fourteen years I've been practicing jiu jitsu. Hundreds of Mondays when I wanted to skip after a long weekend of partying or a wedding or a vacation. It's a terrifying feeling.

Matt gave me one of the greatest gifts that anyone in the world has ever given me: reaching out when I desperately needed someone to be there for me. But he didn't do it once. He didn't do it twice. He did it three times during my blue belt years. Every time I was off the mat for an extended period of time, Matt called me and got me training again.

Toward the end of my blue belt, I became truly serious in my pursuit of jiu jitsu and understood what it would take to go from a hobbyist to a true martial artist. Since I earned my purple belt, I have never taken more than two weeks off at a time from training and only for injuries. When I go on vacation or a business trip, I bring my equipment so I can continue training. I've built relationships with dojos and gyms all over the world where I visit year after year and season after season. Not only do I get to keep up with my training, but I also get to see (and make) jiu jitsu friends.

This moment of fear is something every single person faces, and faces often. You have to have the courage to continue, knowing that it's going to be hard.

Today when I face this feeling after an injury, I ask myself, "Is there any place you'd rather be in the world right now than the dojo?" If your answer is a truthful yes, that's okay. Go do anything else with your life.

More often than not, my truthful answer is no, there is no place I'd rather be. Don't think that's because every training session I have is great. There have been countless times that I've been scared to go because I knew I was going to get beat up. The difference between me-now and me-then is then, I would never have said I was scared. I would have said I was tired, had an important meeting, or needed to focus on my personal life. It's so easy to quit. The devil on your shoulder is whispering to you constantly, "You're tired. It's going to hurt. You have family obligations." You're desperately looking for a reason to give up.

Being able to master your own ego is what starts the process of getting better. You need to recognize this fear in yourself, admit that it's there, and continue anyway. Show up, even when it's hard. Even when you know you're going to get beat up.

Fear of Finishing

So you've started, and you've continued. You've been traveling the path, grappling physically and metaphorically with all the problems of jiu jitsu. Now you need to work on finishing. In Chapter 12, we'll go into much more detail on finishing principles, but for now, let's look at the fear and failure aspects of finishing.

When you practice jiu jitsu, you sweat and bleed and train with the same people every single day, and all kinds of relationships emerge. Some people you'll like, and some people you won't. There will be people you train with easily and people who consider every training session a war. For the most part, everyone in your cohort will improve and move up at a similar rate. The people you're a white belt with, you'll be a blue belt with, and so on (though you'll find that the longer you train, the more people fall off. Very few stick around, as we just discussed).

As you grow and learn with these people, you start to form bonds with them. So many people are surprised to find that after years and years of training, they suddenly can't make themselves take the win. It's sitting there, but they find themselves releasing it or not trying as hard to seize it.

This strange phenomenon is the fear of winning, the fear of finishing. Most of us are familiar with the fear of failure, but few know that the fear of getting what you want can be even more problematic. This happens in business as well. People ask for a promotion or a raise and get it. Now they have to do the work.

This type of fear is rarely talked about, yet it's an incredibly important part of the dynamics of training environments. If you want to get better at jiu jitsu, I highly encourage you to train with a variety of people, not just the ones in your dojo. I love going to new gyms and training with strangers *because* it's hard.

I've found that some gym owners love to put guests through the wringer with cardio workouts: a hundred pushups, a hundred squats, and a hundred air jumps. They're trying—and usually succeeding—to get you tired. Then, they put you up against a huge competitor. However, you don't know what you're walking into in each new academy.

That fear in your mind is what's keeping you from succeeding. When you can get over the fear and walk into a new gym for the first time, take the skills you've been working on, and employ them against people who don't know your style, strength, and techniques, you experience a moment of extreme growth.

The only thing better than walking into a new gym is competing. Making competition a part of your life is a cheat code in getting better faster. If going on vacation puts you months behind your teammates, training six weeks for a competition and then competing against ten people in your division puts you months ahead of your teammates.

I have been both of these people at different points in my jiu jitsu life. Like business, jiu jitsu does not follow linear growth. It's like a roller coaster: up, down, up, down, setback, plateau, up, down, injury, up, down. It's a constant battle.

When you're training with your teammates you love because you've sweated and bled with them, you owe it to them *and to yourself* to give them everything you have—to try to beat them. It's one of the hardest things to do.

Think of all those movies where the student has to take down the master (Darth Vader versus Palpatine, Batman versus Ra's al Ghul, Gandalf versus Saruman,

Kiddo versus Bill). Usually, the student has an opportunity to win early in the movie but hesitates. But eventually, they get the opportunity to win and take it.

Eventually, you will find yourself on the back of a teammate whose back you have never seen before, your arm around their neck, and you need to finish that choke to win. One of two things will happen: you'll finish the choke, or you won't finish the choke.

Business Principle: Look at Failure from a New Lens

One of the best things about my dad is his natural and learned business philosophy. When I was creeping into my thirties, I was experiencing a lot of success at Mixology, and I was also his chief employee at our real estate company. One day as we were sitting together on vacation in Florida, he looked at me and said, "You know, Jordan, if you ever want to go do anything else, I don't want to hold you back. If you feel like you can run faster and further somewhere else, go do it. Don't think you have to stay at the family business."

I smiled and said, "I appreciate you saying that, but I'm exactly where I want to be. This is what I want to do. Anything I accomplish, I'm going to accomplish here, on behalf of our family."

That conversation reminded me of another. It was 2008, and it felt like the world was ending because of the Great Recession. My dad told me, "One day, you and your friends are going to push my generation out of the way." Reading those words, it's easy to think he sounded bitter or resigned. But instead, he sounded hopeful and proud.

What he was saying without saying it was that when people get power, it can be hard for them to share or give it up when their time is past. You can look at our country's leaders to see an example. Back in the day, companies practiced forced retirement when you turned sixty. In 2024, we have an eighty-one-year-old running the country. The average age of a senator is sixty-five years old.[19]

My dad's style of mentorship was never to do it for me and never to show me how. It was to guide me with principled decision-making filtered through my core values; it was to share with me his core values, tell me stories, and then let me figure it out on my own. He let me make my own decisions and face my own fears my entire life.

When I was in high school and into college, I paid my own bills. He never showed me how to balance a checkbook. He never showed me how to pay a mortgage. When I was eighteen, I bought my first apartment in Boston, pre-recession when they were giving out mortgages to anyone who asked, and I figured out the whole process by myself.

---

[19] Carrie Blazina and Drew DeSilver, "House Gets Younger, Senate Gets Older: A Look at the Age and Generation of Lawmakers in the 118th Congress," Pew Research Center, January 31, 2023, https://www.pewresearch.org/short-reads/2023/01/30/house-gets-younger-senate-gets-older-a-look-at-the-age-and-generation-of-lawmakers-in-the-118th-congress/.

If I came to ask him questions, he would tell me to figure it out and make the mistakes on my own—and I made plenty of mistakes.

Fear of Starting

Take the Boston apartment, for example. The apartment was a brownstone located just outside the campus of Northeastern University on a beautiful, tree-lined street. I kept telling him, "We need to buy an apartment in Boston. This is going to be an investment. I'm telling you, this apartment is going to pay for my college education by the time I graduate. The mortgage is going to be cheaper than the rent. I'll bring in a roommate to offset the costs."

Even then, I was real estate obsessed, but I had no real-life experience in it yet. I was a real estate white belt.

Finally, he looked at me and said, "Jordan, if you want to do it, go do it. What do you need me for?" So I started talking to a mortgage broker. At the time, you only had to put a small amount of money down for a mortgage. I put $38,500 down for a mortgage on a gorgeous two-bedroom apartment (10 percent of the purchase price of $385,000). My mother helped me decorate. My roommate, Sam Zises, moved in, and every month I paid the electric and cable bills with the rent he paid me.

Every quarter, I received tax bills for the apartment, and every quarter, I opened them, closed them, and put them in a drawer, telling myself, "I'll pay it next month." The tax bills kept piling up, and I kept putting them in the drawer—except now they stayed unopened.

One year went by. Then two. Every time I received a new bill, my fear increased. I was trying to hide the fear in a drawer.

Finally, after almost three years, I decided this had to stop because it was going to become a major problem. I called the number on the bill and made up a white lie about changing addresses. "I wanted to check how much I owed on the taxes."

"You don't owe any taxes," she replied. "All of your taxes are current."

I was shocked. "Something must be wrong. Who's paying them?"

"It's part of your mortgage escrow. Every month when you make your mortgage payment, the mortgage company sends in the taxes," she explained.

Eight million pounds magically fell off of me. In an instant, I went from hiding from this terrifying, looming fear that was eating at me to being unafraid to open the mail for the first time in years. I learned an unbelievable lesson: don't be fearful of the unknown; take care of problems immediately. Just start.

I cannot stress how lucky I was in this situation. Sometimes in life, luck can save you. However, you have to treat luck as a teacher and learn from the mistake luck saved you from. I only needed to learn this lesson one time because afterward, I did not repeat this mistake again. I never wanted to feel that pit in my stomach again.

As a business owner with experience, I've also learned that there is going to be a point in business when you need to stop asking questions. There's nothing wrong with consulting mentors, taking courses, and reading books, but at some point, you have to make a decision, act on it, and live with the consequences.

Fear of Continuing

Business is a daily grind. When you finish a deal, it's easy to fall into the trap of wanting a break. To be successful, you need to always have something waiting in your pipeline. When my dad sold his family business, All Metro Health Care, in 2005, he moved to the next business, Chart Organization, the next day—because he had started Chart in 2003, two years earlier.

So many people who win the lottery stop working and then spend every single dime. People who close a big deal or sell their business take their foot off the pedal and begin to slow down. They lose their momentum.

In business, you should constantly be thinking about your next move. Jeff Bezos said, "None of the people who report to me should really be focused on the current quarter. When I have a good quarterly conference call with Wall Street, people will stop me and say, 'Congratulations on your quarter,' and I say, 'Thank you,' but what I'm really thinking is that quarter was baked three years ago. You need to be thinking two or three years in advance."[20]

You want to be thinking about and working on the momentum ahead, and that can be terrifying. It's the kind of fear that most are not willing to even admit to themselves. Yes, you closed that big deal, but what's next? You have to show up and perform again tomorrow.

On July 6, 2019, UFC welterweight Jorge Masvidal had one great flying knee on Ben Askren, knocking him out instantly in the first five seconds of the fight. It was incredible, but guess what. He had to show up in the next fight. Winning is not about the one-punch knockout. It's about getting up every single day and training to gain that 1 percent improvement.

The fear of continuing is underreported and misunderstood. It's the daily battle you fight with yourself to get out of bed on time, do the pushups, go on the twenty-minute run, and do the work. All of these daily battles have fear associated with them, and most people are unwilling to recognize it.

One of the easiest ways to get a customer to come back is to write them a thank-you note. It takes two minutes out of your day to write, "Hey, Adam! I hope that date you were going on went well. Thank you so much for supporting our small business. I've always got your back. Please come back anytime."

I receive so few genuine thank-you notes in

---

[20] Jeff Bezos, "Thinking Three Years out - Fast Company," Fast Company, November 23, 2020, https://www.fastcompany.com/90578272/how-jeff-bezos-makes-decisions.

business that when I do, it creates a real, authentic, amazing relationship. My best employees do this. My worst employees never do it. When I'm coaching a bottom performer, they refuse to believe increasing repeat sales from customers is as easy as a genuine thank-you note. They try to find the "real" secret to success.

One of my best team members is Crystal Cagno (from Chapter 1). For the past few years, she has been in the number-one slot on our Salesforce ARC leaderboard and number one in sales performance. And she writes thank-you notes to every single person who buys from her. She takes that first step to create relationships with all of her customers. Now, any time they're near the store, they stop by to say hi.

I'm not saying a thank-you note will work for every single customer. But that doesn't mean you stop writing them altogether. The fear of continuing wins when you try something once or twice (or three or ten times), and it doesn't work, so you give up. Guess what. It might take you three years, like building ARC did.

Ideas rarely see success in one day. But when you have a good idea that you pursue with conviction and dedication, trying and trying and trying again, you'll eventually find success. It can take years of hard work. It's easy to watch a UFC fight; it's not easy to step into the ring and win the fight.

In business and jiu jitsu, you have to keep coming back every single day, trying and improving, trying and improving. It's a constant daily grind to get better, and your ideas can take years to manifest. You have to be able to conquer your fear of starting and continuing every day in order to succeed, which is hard in normal circumstances. In 2020, it was much harder.

Fear and Failure during COVID

At this point in COVID, I had created and enacted our emergency action plan, relying on muscle memory to make the right decisions. But I had to overcome a lot of fear to make these decisions.

When things are coming at you left and right and you're carrying the weight of decision-making for your company, it's natural to be paralyzed by fear. To overcome it, you have to first accept it. "It's normal for me to be scared right now."

When I experience this fear, as I did during COVID, I like to think about the history of my ancestors and the great people I admire and put myself in their shoes. I told myself, "Look at what other people have had to go through. Now I'm going through something unprecedented, except I have all these resources available to me. I have my car. I have cash in the bank. I have my team. I have a house I can go to."

I was able to detach from my fear by counting the resources I had at my disposal versus focusing on what had been taken away from me. Once I could step away from my fear, I was able to make decisions from a place of measured calm. If you don't detach yourself from fear, you make bad decisions based on panic.

As we moved further into the pandemic, a new type

of fear crept into my life: the fear of making decisions that I knew could come back to haunt me. By choosing to follow COVID protocols, I'd be breaking employment laws of New York State.

At the end of May 2020, physical stores were still forced to be closed by the New York state government, but people were starting to be allowed out of their houses, and some businesses were allowed to start curbside pickup. It was Memorial Day weekend, which is traditionally one of our biggest sales weekends, so I set up a small curbside pickup station in front of our Westhampton Beach store.

As customers started showing up, many asked if they could go inside. After three months of being locked inside your home, the novelty of being able to do something normal was very tempting. All the other small stores on the street were letting a few people in at a time, so I decided it wouldn't hurt to let one person in at a time.

Then, a police officer drove up. He approached me, wearing full tactical gear, very frustrated, and said, "You're allowed to do curbside pickup." He pointed to where I was sitting on the porch of my store. "Is that a curb? Or is it a porch?"

"It's a porch, sir," I replied.

"It's curbside pickup, not porch-side pickup," he said. He was angry that people were walking up onto the porch to get their orders. After a minute, he got back in his cruiser, but he didn't drive away. He sat in it, right in front of the store, and stared at me until a few customers walked up. The customers took two steps onto the porch, and the cop stormed out of his car.

"You are the reason we're going to have an outbreak," he yelled at me. "I'm shutting you down, putting you in handcuffs, and calling the CDC."

Now, I didn't know if he had the ability to do that. But after being in my house for three months, the idea that he could do that was scary. I didn't know if I was going to be able to keep Mixology in business. This was supposed to be one of our biggest weekends of the year, and if we didn't get the business we needed, we weren't going to survive.

I said, "No problem, sir." I turned to the customers and very politely asked them to leave. Then I turned back to him, looked him in the eye, and said, "Officer, I know that you're under a lot of stress. I am too. I don't think I'm the reason there's going to be an outbreak, but I'll tell you what I'm going to do. If these women walking up and standing on my porch make you feel like you have to put me in handcuffs, I'm going to close down my store. I don't want to put you in this position, and I certainly don't want to be in that position." I closed and locked the door and went home.

The learnings of jiu jitsu teach you counterintuitive steps that most people are not doing. When met with a force or action, they give an equal and opposite reaction. When someone yells at you, most people's natural instinct is to either be dominated or yell back. If a police officer is dominating them, they're either going to tuck their tail between their legs or battle back. More often than not, people choose the latter. Jiu jitsu gave me another option. I didn't tuck my tail or become combative. I decided to find a different way to win: defusing the situation.

Still, I felt totally defeated, like my balloon had burst. Up to this point, it had been three months of trying to get $300 per employee per day. This was our first chance to get out of our houses and earn big money to get back on track—and the one guy had popped my excitement bubble. I could feel a cloud of fear and failure descending on me.

But because of my many years of training, I was able to see through the fog. I told myself that this situation wasn't about me, and it wasn't about him. Focusing on how upset I was wouldn't help me or my employees. I needed to focus on how to get back to winning. Pushing away the fear and failure associated with getting shut down gave me the snap I needed to get back on offense.

This situation would have been enough to make anyone want to give up, especially after being beaten down for so many months and working so hard to keep your people employed. An encounter like this makes you feel like a victim. When you've been made to feel like a victim by something outside your control, it's difficult to coach yourself to detach from the situation, come back to reality, and decide, "This encounter is not going to be the reason I don't win. If I can't do it this way, I'll win another way."

Dealing with Lawsuits
I could have taken the situation further and sued the

police or the city for being shut down that day, but I decided it wasn't worth the trouble. I'm not litigious; I don't sue. It's tempting to say, "I'm going to sue you!" but it's almost never a good route. It's messy, and typically, unless you are extremely wronged, the only people who win are the lawyers. Let your actions speak louder than your words, and make lawsuits your last option.

Dealing with lawsuits is rarely talked about publicly in the business world. But the truth is, people suing you on a regular basis when you own a business (or have any kind of prominence) is commonplace because of the way our legal system and governmental bureaucracy work. In fact, the average citizen is encouraged to sue companies. All you have to do is turn on the TV in the evening, and you'll see ad after ad from lawyers: "Did you work overtime?" "Did you slip and fall?" "Have you been in a car accident?"

These lawyers are spending millions of dollars advertising to convince people that it's okay to sue. They'll get people to sue for every law, from employment, age, gender, and sexual orientation discrimination to the Americans With Disabilities Act (ADA). For every law created, there's someone who wants to exploit it (which ruins them for the people these laws were intended to help).

The first time I was sued, it felt like somebody took a knife and stabbed me right in the heart. It felt like the weight of the world was crashing down on me. "Why would someone sue me?" I asked my dad. "I didn't do anything wrong."

My very wise dad said, **"This isn't about you.** Of course you didn't do anything wrong. This is about them. They want money."

Early in my career, while I was primarily working in the real estate business, I was mostly sued over slip-and-falls. "Joe Smith slipped and fell at your property on February 14." The most interesting aspect of these lawsuits is that they rarely go to trial. They usually settle out of court. That's because we're insured for most of these types of lawsuits, and the lawyers know this, so they demand an amount just under the amount it would cost the insurance company to take the case to trial. The insurance company doesn't want to go to court, so they settle for that amount. It becomes a smart business decision because both the lawyers and insurance companies know that it's cheaper to settle for $80,000 than it is to pay $250,000 in legal fees. There's a certain subset of average people who know this, and they sue over and over and over again, actually making their living by suing companies. It is pathetic. It is wrong.

Throughout the early days of my career into the midpoint of my career, these lawsuits ate up so much of my time, energy, and mental capacity, because I was playing the victim too. I eventually came to realize this was another type of fear: the fear of being taken advantage of.

I have read hundreds of books and taken dozens of classes, but I had never heard of this perspective—until I stumbled across a YouTube video of Will Smith called "The Truth of Being Famous." In the video, Smith reveals he gets sued an average of fifteen times a year. He talked about them in the same way I was feeling: he didn't know these people. They came out of the woodwork.

I finally realized that, like the cop's anger, most of these lawsuits are not about me. They're not about my business. They are simply obstacles. Think about the game Chutes and Ladders: sometimes you land on a chute and have to go back a few spaces. Sometimes when you're in a jiu jitsu match, you get hit with a sweep and have to fight back into neutral.

When an unhappy event happens, it should be viewed as part of the complexity of the game, not a personal attack on you—even though sometimes it is a personal attack on you. In order to make clear, rational decisions, you have to put the event in perspective. Every single time I had to go through a lawsuit, deal with lawyers, and spend hours on the phone, I got better and better and better at dealing with them. And I got less and less fearful.

Don't misunderstand—I still get annoyed every time one lands on my desk. But I want you to know that this is normal. Frustrating, yes, but normal. The first time, you'll feel like the weight of the world is on your shoulders and that you have to fight this thing tooth and nail.

Instead, consider your legal expense as a business expense, similar to marketing, travel, or inventory. If you become consumed by the fear and uncertainty of these lawsuits, you won't be able to make decisions and grow your business. And the simple fact is that your job as the business owner is to grow the business. Getting caught up in the details of these frivolous cases will drag your whole business down. Do you want to drag a multimillion-dollar business down over a $15,000 or even $80,000 lawsuit?

I could let these lawsuits upset me. I could dwell on them and let them distract me from growing my companies.

Instead, I remember a lesson from the movie *A Bronx Tale:*

A young man spots Calogero 'C' Anello and starts sprinting in the other direction.

C: He owes me twenty dollars. It's been two weeks now, and every time he sees me he keeps dodging me. He's becoming a real pain in the ass. Should I crack him one or what?

Sonny: Sometimes hurting somebody ain't the answer. First of all, is he a good friend of yours?

C: No. I don't even like him.

Sonny: You don't even like him. There's your answer right there. Look at it this way: it costs you twenty dollars to get rid of him...he's out of your life for twenty dollars. you got off cheap. Forget him.[21]

---

[21] Robert De Niro, dir. A Bronx Tale. 1993; Price Entertainment and TriBeCa Productions, 1993.

As a business owner, you need to stop looking at the world through the lens of how people are hurting you or screwing you over, and instead look through the lens of how they are helping you or doing you a favor. If you can look at every single obstacle as a potential move forward, you can begin to see that you're not failing. When you get sued, you're creating opportunities for growth.[22]

Pete Roberts, CEO and founder of Origin USA, told me to consider mistakes and obstacles, like lawsuits, **business tuition**.[23] It's no different than paying college tuition: you pay for a class, and you learn something. When a police officer shuts down your curbside business, no problem: tuition payment. When someone sues you even though you did nothing wrong, no problem: tuition payment.

Understand that I've learned these lessons after years of struggle. I've been through lawsuits where I wanted to cry, ones where I saw red. I've been through times that have taken so much energy out of me that I had to muster every last drop of strength to make it to the other side, similar to a hard training session.

When this happens to you, it's only natural that you feel scared, angry, fearful. It's only when you've been

---

[22] Note: I am referring to frivolous lawsuits that are out of your control, not big cases that happen because your company is doing something shady, unethical, illegal, or immoral. I mean the ones that happen even though you're following your core values, following the law, and performing to the best of your abilities.

[23] Episode 45: Pete Roberts | Origin: Made in America

through these situations countless times that you can have the kind of clarity I've talked about in this chapter. You're going to be fearful. You're going to fail, but know that those times are going to be the fuel that takes you to the next level. I hope this chapter not only helps you see your situation from a different perspective but helps you feel less alone. You're not the only person who has been through this. I have too.

There are things that will always be outside of your control. When you are dealing with loss, it's your choice to decide when and if you are defeated.[24]

It comes down to endurance. Are you able to endure the pain of your ego being checked, of looking and feeling embarrassed, and still show up again and again? Will you fall prey to the blue belt blues?

The people who become incredibly successful in business and jiu jitsu can get their egos bruised without it making them quit. They may stop momentarily, like I did during my blue belt blues, but they still come back. They find the courage to get back on the mat.

Mat Chat

When someone has their arms wrapped around your neck, you know how close that feeling is to the feeling of dying. The way to unlock that trap is with a double tap. When you take that first breath once released, you

---

[24] My favorite book on this topic is *Man's Search for Meaning* by Viktor Frankl, which is about his experience of being a Holocaust prisoner and survivor.

know, whether consciously (if you've been practicing a long time) or subconsciously (if you're just starting out), that we are simulating murder.

If the person were to hold on to that choke for a few moments longer, you would die. The blood and oxygen would be cut off to your brain, and you would never wake up. In the words of my sensei, "We're not baking cupcakes out here." We're training in a martial art. We're training to protect ourselves in life-and-death situations.

However, as the years go on, you can forget the weight of what you're doing because you're so used to your partner tapping. There's no dress rehearsal in a real fight. If someone gets their arms around your neck, they might not let go. The fact that you have this ability to train and learn how to get out of this deadly situation cannot be overstated.

You have to have complete trust that your partner is going to let go of your neck when you tap. In the case of an armbar or heel hook, they are taking your limbs, muscles, and ligaments right up to the breaking point. When you train, you're taking your body and mind to the breaking point—or to the death point. Think about what that does for your ability as a human. Never forget that the training you're doing is to become better.

This is the same view you need to take of your business life too. Whenever you've been brought to the absolute breaking point, whether it's a pandemic, a recession, or a lawsuit, and you do not break, the only feeling you should have on the other side is gratitude that it has propelled you to the next level of your career.

After COVID, Mixology Clothing Company doubled in size. All that struggle and pain we endured, two years of struggle and furloughs and lawsuits and hospital-grade disinfectant and masks, enabled us to grow faster and stronger.

We mastered the fear and the failure and used it as fuel.

Chapter 6
Family and Friends

Travis Stevens is a three-time US Olympian in the art of Judo and a Black Belt in Brazilian jiu jitsu under John Danaher. He won a silver medal in the 2016 Rio de Janeiro games and has had a storied career competing in martial arts. When Travis was on the podcast,[25] he told me about the mentality and lifestyle it takes to win an Olympic medal. He said something that has stuck with me on a daily basis, it was something like, "I don't have anyone in my life, or even know anybody, who would be foolish enough to call me on a Friday night to go out. Because they know I will be getting up early Saturday morning to train."

When you're singularly focused on something great, your family and friends may or may not understand your drive to succeed.

In 2015, two former Navy SEAL officers, Jocko Willink and Leif Babin, coauthored the book *Extreme Ownership*, which teaches readers how to apply the mindset and principles that enable SEAL units to

---

[25] Ep 17: Travis Stevens | Whatever It Takes

accomplish the most difficult missions in combat to families, teams, and organizations. This book had a significant impact on my life. I brought many of the principles over to my business, including making one of Mixology Clothing Company's core values "taking extreme ownership" in honor of the book's impact on me.

Over the following years, Jocko and Leif found that readers were constantly telling them, "I'm taking the most ownership. Nobody's taking more ownership than me. The problem is no one else is taking ownership." So they wrote a follow-up book, *The Dichotomy of Leadership*, in 2018. This book explains the need for balance. The goal is to know how to practice extreme leadership while also giving ownership to your team, when to take aggressive action and when to wait, and when to lead and when to follow.

Being extreme is not about being extreme with other people and expecting them to be you. It's about being extreme with yourself.

When I read these books, I realized that I was blaming my business partners when I was the one who had to change. I needed to figure out the solutions to our challenges. It wasn't incumbent on them to change. I had to change the way I was reacting. I couldn't have a short fuse. I couldn't expect everybody to work as hard as I was. I couldn't hold other people to the same standards I held myself to.

In 2022, I was invited to an Echelon Front event (Jocko and Leif's leadership training company) to sit in on a leadership seminar being hosted for first responders, police officers, and firefighters. The attendees were allowed to bring one civilian guest, and my friend and podcast guest Mike Conicelli, who is a jiu jitsu athlete, bar owner, and NYFD firefighter, invited me.[26]

While the entire seminar was incredible, my favorite speaker was JP Dinnel, a retired Navy SEAL from Jocko's unit in Iraq (he later came on my podcast[27]). I expected to learn about battlefield tactics and how to use SEAL principles in both business and the line of duty. JP stood up in front of a room of 200 of the toughest state police, firefighters, and EMTs and said, "Before I talk to you about extreme ownership in your job, I'm going to talk to you about the most important thing in your life: your personal relationships."

This is not a topic you typically hear Navy SEALs and tough men discuss. JP explained why extreme ownership is more important in the home than anywhere else and how to take extreme ownership in your life.

In JP's words, he had the best job in the world: shooting guns, jumping out of airplanes, taking down bad guys, storming buildings, and riding in Humvees. But when his military career was over, he went home to a marriage—his third—that was falling apart. He told

---

[26] Ep 10: Mike Conicelli | How to Lead & Adopting a Beginner's Mindset

[27] Ep 54: JP Dinnell | Former Navy Seal and BJJ Athlete

us how he was an absolute mess, and he realized he needed to get his life together. He needed to take his life into his own hands—take extreme ownership. He did and completely reinvented his life: he started dating his wife again, went back to church, got a new job working at Echelon, and fixed his health.

Nick Koumalatsos is another example of a military member who struggled once he retired.[28] When serving as a Marine Raider in MARSOC, the special operations wing of the Marines, every moment of his life was scripted from the moment he woke up: when and what he ate, when and how he trained, where he went, etc. He went from operating at the level of a professional athlete to being unmoored. Nick became suicidal in his loneliness until he realized other retired military members might be feeling the same way.

Like JP, he went on a journey to find meaning in a post-military life. He wrote a book about his journey called *Excommunicated Warrior: 7 Stages of Transition*, took up jiu jitsu, started a podcast, and launched several successful businesses.

You can be an incredible businessperson or incredible at jiu jitsu. But in my opinion, the goal is not to have extreme ownership over only one part of your life. Many SEALS, professional athletes, and billionaires focus intently on a single area of their lives, and in doing so, they become the best in the world at what they do. The rest of their lives, however, are in shambles. The goal is to find a way to master your

---

[28] Ep 33: Nick Koumalatsos | Always Forward

whole life, from the moment you wake up until the moment you fall asleep. To do that, it's useful to understand all the different aspects of your life, especially your closest personal relationships.

In my life at work, I'm the boss and leader. At home and at jiu jitsu, I'm a member of the team. In order to be successful, you have to be able to weave in and out of different parts of your life where sometimes you're the leader and sometimes you're the follower.

Even when you're not the head boss, you should be able to be a great leader. Many people ask, "But how can you have extreme ownership if you're just a member of the team?" Jocko and Leif make the argument that leadership is not about being the leader or president or CEO. Leadership is embodying these philosophies no matter who you are on the team, even if you're the most junior person and even at the dinner table.

Often, people who own businesses and are the leaders of their families become consumed by power and control. Everything is about them. Every decision has to go through them. They dominate their work, and they dominate their families. They can't handle any part of their life where they have to be a member of a team. They think everyone is an idiot, they are always wrong, or they're a bad teammate.

In the book *Elon Musk* by Walter Isaacson, Walter mentions that during his time interviewing Elon Musk, Steve Jobs, and other prominent innovators, he noticed they would often lose patience, blow up, and yell the same line: "That is the dumbest thing I have ever heard in my life." After reading that, I began to realize that I've used that line myself (too often for comfort). My younger brother, Tyler, has called me out for saying this often. I would throw the line out during dinner, and Tyler would calmly respond, "Really? It's the stupidest thing you've ever heard in your entire life?" His kind and noncombative nature made the criticism hit home even harder.

It's a line that doesn't consider that something that comes easily to you doesn't come easily to other people. It's important to cultivate empathy by considering the experiences and challenges of others, recognizing that what may seem straightforward to us could be difficult for them.

The truth is you're not always going to be the star of your show, even when it's your business. There's a saying: "It's all on you, but it's not all about you." Alternatively, your whole life can become about taking extreme ownership and finding balance. But it's not all about you, even if it's your company, your household, or your charitable organization. The moment you bring in outside stakeholders of any kind—employees, investors, partners, significant others, children—it's not about you anymore.

Jiu Jitsu Principle: Be a Good Member of Your Academy

People come into your life for all kinds of reasons. Sometimes you have a friend who is a great party friend. You want to go to Vegas for the weekend? He's there. But don't expect him to show up for your son's first birthday party.

I've been that friend. When I was single and my friends started having children, I'd RSVP yes to a kid's birthday party, go out the night before, and wake up in the morning hungover and unwilling to drive out to the suburbs for the party. Many times I didn't even bother to call or text. It wasn't until I was a father that I realized how wrong what I did was. I did, however, know to expect it to happen to me. And when it did, I could acknowledge that my friend was in a different part of their life, and no ill will was meant.

In my single days, I also put a lot of pressure on my best married friends, Ryann and Scott Lorberbaum (the same friend I mentioned in Chapter 1). At the time, they had recently had their first child and were living in the city. I would call them, saying, "Let's go out to dinner. Get a sitter." They'd try to decline, and I'd keep badgering them, putting pressure on them to spend time with me. It wasn't until I had my first child that I realized what I had been doing: pressuring two people who were exhausted and overwhelmed taking care of an infant to spend their nonexistent energy going out with me. Two years later when I found myself in their position, I called them to apologize, and they very graciously accepted and laughed at me.

Being able to cultivate great relationships with people requires you to understand their perspective and what they're going through in life, even if you haven't been through those events yet. The most successful people I've encountered are able to recognize when they're being the jerk. I've had to learn to take a deep breath in challenging situations, ask myself if I'm in the wrong, and then answer myself honestly. When I answer yes, I remind myself that I'm learning and growing. People who grow, evolve, and learn from their mistakes find a lot of success. Sadly, even in my late twenties, I had people reporting to me who were two or three times my age making the same mistakes and taking the same actions over and over again.

Some of these people were parents of friends. I looked up to these people as a kid, thinking they were smart and powerful. Now they were working for me, making the mistakes of a teenager. There's a saying that when you're a kid looking up at adults, first you idolize them. Then, as a teenager, you demonize them. Finally, as an adult yourself, you humanize them. You realize they're people just like you, simply trying to figure life out—just like you.

One of the biggest factors affecting your ability to build great relationships is being able to empathize with what the other person is going through, not what you're going through. In *The 7 Habits of Highly Effective People*, Stephen Covey explains the fifth habit is to seek first to understand and then to be understood, which is the key to empathetic communication. The first time I read that, I was blown away by how powerful a statement it was. Unfortunately, when I've shared this advice with others who need it, the common response is to shrug it off.

This is why jiu jitsu is so powerful. The people who

choose to practice jiu jitsu have accepted that they will live a life in a constant state of learning. They're going to keep learning to improve their life, even if they're forty, fifty, or sixty. The people who can't learn from their mistakes will never progress to the next belt. They refuse to learn, so they never advance.

Business Principle: The Ups and Downs of Family

At this point in the book, we've talked about the importance of implementing a technical framework to create muscle memory and of constant learning. We've talked about creating and utilizing an emergency action plan. We've talked about finding neutral and going on the attack. We've talked about feeling and overcoming fear. But fear isn't the only emotion you're going to feel.

Entrepreneurship can often feel isolating. Surprisingly, some of the people you'd expect to be your strongest supporters—even those closest to you such as parents or siblings—might not always have your back. Some individuals might use this lack of support as a reason (or an excuse) for potential failure, while also believing they deserve unwavering support, as if they're the center of the universe.

This chapter explains why you shouldn't be a spoiled brat and, instead, be empathetic to what the rest of the people in your life are going through. We'll also discuss why the people closest to you act the way they do: your parents and your siblings are always going to see you as a little kid.

Many psychologists say your base self is developed in your toddler years, usually around the age of four or five, and that programming will stay with you for the rest of your life. However, in the Jewish community, we believe you become an adult at age thirteen. That edge, when you're beginning your teenage years and leaving your adolescence, is what I consider to be the time of the base self. You have to decide for yourself where that line is, but the easiest way to decide is to think about the age of your inner child—the age of the person you regress to when you're feeling sad, lonely, or insecure.

The base self is extremely easy to fall back on in times of stress. The goal of jiu jitsu and constant learning is to improve—to overcome the base self. By reshaping and remolding yourself, hopefully, you will become strong enough that targeted comments from your siblings, parents, or even a stranger on the street cannot trigger you into your base self. Of everything we need to learn in life, mastering our base self may be the most challenging.

You may have fooled the world—you may have even fooled yourself—but the inability to maintain composure around the dinner table with family, especially while enduring hardships, raises the question: have you really mastered yourself?

After all, family life is one of the most crucial aspects of your existence. This extends not only to your immediate family and extended family but also to the people in your life who are as close as family. Tim

Sanders once said, "Your network is your net worth." Jim Rohn said, "You're the average of the five people you spend most of your time with."

Most people hear these types of quotes and advocate for cutting out negative forces in your life. I don't believe that is always the best move. Sometimes, it does have to be done, especially when your physical or mental well-being is in jeopardy. But generally speaking, running away from a problem or cutting people out of your life is not the answer, the same way you can't decide to skip a hurricane. You don't always get a choice in the matter.

If you're always running away from your problems, you become ill equipped to solve problems. Sometimes the people who are the closest part of your life are the most challenging to have great relationships with. If they're good people and the issue is normal family drama, the solution is learning to let it go. My dad always says, "If you're experiencing drama, reach out your arms to both sides—you'll find the cause of the drama in the center of them." Spoiler: it's you. You are the problem, not them. They aren't perfect either, but that's their journey to discover. You can only focus on yours.

In 2014, my dad happened to see Tony Robbins one morning on CNBC promoting his new book *Money: Master the Game* and suggested I read it. After the 2008 Great Recession, Robbins interviewed the top fifty financial minds of the time to create a playbook for navigating the world of finance. My father is not a self-help guy and did not have any strong opinions on Tony

Robbins. He simply thought I would enjoy learning from all these great finance leaders.

However, Robbins didn't jump straight into the financial advice on page one. In the same vein as JP explained he had to teach us to address our personal life before battlefield tactics, Tony explained that before he could teach you about finance, he needed to teach you about yourself and explain his very simple philosophy.[29]

One tenant of his philosophy is that "success leaves clues." People who are successful leave a trail of breadcrumbs for you to follow. Another tenant is that "where focus goes, energy flows." He explained that the things you think about are the things you're going to manifest.

These books started me on the path of discovery and change—of alchemy.

One of my favorite books is *The Alchemist*. I read it for the first time in 2015, on the recommendation of my (now) wife. It teaches you how to find your personal legend and evolve into who and what you are supposed to be.

Prior to reading Tony's book, I would not have been able to attract my wife. I had recently left a long-term college relationship that was very toxic. I was living the bachelor life in New York City. I was the type of person who thought they deserved things simply because they

---

[29] Tony Robbins, *MONEY Master the Game: 7 Simple Steps to Financial Freedom*. New York: Simon & Schuster Paperbacks, 2014.

existed. Then I read Tony's book and learned that success leaves clues, that where focus goes, energy flows, and realized I was the asshole.

It wasn't my parents, my siblings, or my partners; it was me. I already knew I had to show up for jiu jitsu, and I knew I had to show up for work. I now knew that I had to show up socially too. Not long after, I met my wife at the birthday party of a mutual friend. On our first date, we realized we were both fans of Tony Robbins's book, and she told me about her favorite book, *The Alchemist*.

At this point in my life, I had lived through Hurricane Sandy. I was learning from some of the best leaders in business and jiu jitsu and using those learnings to improve. My love for reading was flourishing and leading me to evolve and grow on a personal level. I met my wife, who helped me move even farther down the path of self-discovery.

All of this was beginning to culminate in success. Mixology Clothing Company grew from $4 million to $8 million. I got engaged and then married. I had discovered my core values and was doing my best to live them every day. Yet something very interesting happened.

The people who have known us for a very long time, especially family and close friends, often have a lasting impression of us based on who we were as young children. Even as we grow, evolve, and change, their perceptions remain rooted in who we were during our formative years or during specific memorable phases of our lives. This can lead them, sometimes unintentionally, to touch upon our deepest insecurities or past vulnerabilities.

Changing perceptions is one of the biggest challenges we face when it comes to long-standing relationships. After all, they know all the skeletons in your closet. They get to decide to pick on you whenever they want. When they make that decision, you have to be the most empathetic to them. Remember that they are only human.

If you're not careful, you will immediately regress to your base self and lose all that work you did. All those books you read and all the success you earned will mean nothing if you fall back into the patterns you had when you were fifteen or twelve or seven. Use all the knowledge you've acquired, and detach from what they're doing or saying (a key principle of extreme ownership). Be the bigger person. Don't let your buttons be pushed. When you can do that, you have truly mastered yourself.

However, while you want great relationships for the sake of having great relationships and practicing self-mastery, don't use a lack of support as an excuse for why you're not winning. It's common to expect your friends and family to have your back no matter what, and they may not. Sometimes they do have your back behind your back. They brag about you to everyone when you're not there, but around the dinner table, they bring you back to your base self.

At the end of the day, you can't use them riling you up as an excuse to not succeed. I've seen it happen often in both work and jiu jitsu when someone's having a bad day and they feel like giving up and all they need is a metaphorical hug—but the person on the other side of the table is not willing to give it. In fact, they beat the person up a little bit more by pushing their buttons. Many give up or walk away.

Over the years, my family has often seen my devotion to jiu jitsu as an annoyance. Jiu jitsu is for me, not for my whole family. There have been times when family members have said, "Shouldn't you be with your kids or focusing on work?" or "Are you still doing that karate thing?" It has nothing to do with my kids (they're usually not even awake when I'm at jiu jitsu, as I often go late at night and early in the morning). It has more to do with their own frustrations needing an outlet.

As we explore different dynamics in the rest of this chapter, remember that it's not about you being a good son or daughter or partner. You should be that, yes, but it's also remembering to detach when these frustrations are directed at you so you can still win.

Mirror Concept

The mirror concept is seen in any power dynamic, but I find it often shows between fathers and sons or mothers and daughters. When a father is overly critical or loses his temper with his son, it reveals more about his own insecurities and unresolved issues than the son's actions.

This harsh behavior can stem from the father's past struggles, desires for his son's future, or traits he sees in his son that mirror his younger self. Such dynamics might perpetuate negative cycles, as fathers unconsciously project their own challenges onto their sons. Awareness and open communication are essential for breaking these patterns and fostering healthier relationships.

I've had to learn this lesson the hard way with my own father. My dad has been hard on me over the years, and every time I've come home angry, my wife gently reminds me, "You are his mirror. He's not saying those things to you. He's saying those things to himself. Those are his own insecurities of things he's not doing or things that he figured out that you're not doing. It has nothing to do with you, but it can come out really, really mean."

Don't get me wrong: I have an incredible relationship with my dad. We wrote a book about our first ten years in business together. He is an amazing businessman and an amazing mentor. However, I also know that I don't want to do to my employees what my dad did to me.

Family Dynamics

My brother-in-law, Jared Schwadron, is on a team of realtors in New York City. Each year from 2019 through 2023, they sold over a billion dollars' worth of residential real estate. But for the three months in 2020 when the world shut down, his business was essentially halted. Instead of relaxing, he fully committed himself to helping my sister and me with Mixology Clothing Company. I can't overstate what it feels like to have someone close to you saying, "I have your back," in the hardest of times—someone who wants to help you carry the load.

In the first days of COVID, Jared was incredibly helpful. He told us, "Whatever you need me to do, I'll do." He didn't know anything about the clothing business. He didn't know anything about the fashion business. But he was willing to do whatever it took to help us. Jared proved you can be a beginner who doesn't know what they're doing and still spring into action and help people. You might be going out of your comfort zone or think you're stepping on people's toes (and he did), but if you are helping out of a genuine desire to be of service, then you should take the risk.

Jared was my friend before he ever met my sister. One of my favorite things about Jared that I saw from the very beginning of our friendship was that he embodies the principle of being of service. He's the guy who's always happy to jump on the barbecue, the one who is always willing to run to Costco. He'll do anything on behalf of his friends and family. If you're going to be stuck in your house during a global pandemic, Jared is the person you want to be with.

Jared not only threw his whole self into helping Mixology, but he was also incredibly supportive of Gabrielle when their wedding plans were thrown into question. They were supposed to be married on a Greek island in June 2020. As the date crept closer and closer, it became more and more clear they were going to have to cancel the wedding. My sister was devastated.

As I mentioned before, my entire family was living in my parents' house in the Hamptons: me, my wife, my infant son, and our son's Nanny, Gloria; my cousin Jill; my brother Tyler and his wife, Jess; my parents; and Jared and Gabrielle. It was the first time my siblings and I had lived together since I was fourteen and left for boarding school.

While in a sad situation, Jared showed me what a partner who is truly there for their significant other acts like. He was sad and depressed, too, but my sister was in a deep, dark depression. For many people, their wedding is one of the biggest days of their life. Gabrielle was heartbroken that her dream wedding was being taken away from her. Jared not only made sure she was taking care of herself—eating, exercising, drinking water—but he also started helping her with her work. When she didn't even want to get out of bed because of her depression, he helped her up, helped her get on the Zoom calls, and helped her lead her team.

He also helped her develop her voice. Before COVID, Gabrielle ran Mixology's buying department, and she didn't have much crossover or communication with the other departments. With Jared's help, she started to develop more confidence. She stepped into her own voice. He would sit in on calls with her and, afterward, coach her on how she could improve. It was beautiful to witness their relationship blossom and grow even more while we lived together. While Jared didn't always know what he was doing, he lit a fire under the employees, showing them what it would take to save the business. He also became heavily involved in the creative process, getting the stores open, getting them cleaned, and sanitized.

Jared is incredibly meticulous—he has to be in order to sell $10–$20 million apartments. His eye for excellence is unwavering, with a focus on the details. As a small business owner, however, I don't have $10 million to invest in a single store. I have a $250,000 budget. What Jared taught us was that the pitch of a light or the placement of a plant can have an underrated effect on the feel of a store. He showed us how to have a $10 million store on a $250,000 budget.

Like me, Gabby was working early in the morning until late at night. She took over the creative team, working with them to ensure our website was fine-tuned, as well as reporting on sales each day so we would have our mobile Salesforce leaderboard ready for the next morning's call. Her work ensured that when I started our morning Zoom, I knew who our hero was for the day, what marketing campaigns were most effective, and what we needed to do that day.

We were all working extremely hard during the day, but around six thirty at night, we all migrated down from our individual rooms and get ready for dinner. Tyler, Jared, Jill, and Gloria cooked us amazing meals, and the entire family sat around the table for a family dinner every single night. My son, Axel, who was only one year of age at the time, gained eight more parents while we lived there. In a dark time, his wonder and innocence were a breath of fresh air for all of us (Gabby would often say that Axel saved her during that difficult year).

However, not every single night was rosy. There were nights when it was really hard. Some nights, people didn't want to show up to the dinner table because they were mad at someone, they had a terrible day, or the weight of the uncertainty in the world was weighing them down. There were arguments. There were nights when someone skipped out on cleaning the dishes and someone else was resentful.

There were hard conversations too. My wife had to return to the city because she was finishing her surgical residency, and the hospital called up all the doctors and residents to help with the overwhelming number of COVID patients. She went from being a podiatry resident in the orthopedics department to a COVID doctor tending to patients. When she returned to Manhattan, I didn't know when I would see her again. At the time, scientists were far away from a vaccine, and no one knew the odds of dying if you contracted the disease. She was devastated that she wasn't going to be able to see our son, her baby, for an unknown amount of time.

We had to ask ourselves what we would do in a dozen situations. What if she contracted it and died? What if she contracted it and I had to come take care of her? What if she came to visit on the weekend and brought it into the house? Should she be allowed to come home on the weekends? These hard conversations became friction points with some of the family. Some members were fine with her coming home on the weekends, while others were scared and didn't want anyone who left to come back in.

These are the kinds of dynamics that exist within families that you need to be aware of, and while it can be hard, you have to practice understanding and empathy. I told my wife that we shouldn't hold it against anyone for how they felt. Everyone was terrified, and we didn't have the answers right then. I told her to go back to the city and that we would make the best decisions we could when we had more information. Jared, bless him, paid a fortune out of his own pocket to have doctors make house calls on a regular basis to test the family and bring everyone comfort.

Remember the saying, "It's all on you, but it's not all about you." Knowing my wife was on the front lines and the rest of the family was living comfortably in a big house, it was hard to sit around the dinner table and ask, "How are you?" Some of them didn't have people's lives at stake. They didn't have to make payroll that week or have dozens of rent checks to write. They simply had to show up for their job and collect their paycheck. I couldn't expect them to know what I was going through.

And at the same time, who cared what I was going through? I was not the only person in the world to own a business. I was not the only one going through a hard time. I was not the only one who was stressed about the unknowns and uncertainties with family members on the front line.

I don't know who in the house had the least on their plate, but I can guarantee that they felt the same feelings and pressures I did. The amount of responsibility you have or what you have at stake doesn't matter to the other people in your life because we're all having our own human experience. As Joe Rogan often says, "The worst thing a person has ever been through is the worst thing they have ever been through."

Yes, my wife was on the front lines. Yes, I had an infant son at home. Yes, I was trying to keep a company alive. But when I showed up at the dinner table, I had to get over myself and recognize that every other person at that table was living through their own human experience—and theirs was just as serious as mine.

In war, there's the front-line infantry troops, and there's the cook, and there's the clerk. Everyone has a different role to play. You need to be able to empathize with everyone's situation without judging anyone's situation. You don't know why they're in that position. The front-line soldier may belittle the clerk only to find out they lost their leg on the front lines but wanted to stay and help with the war effort.

You have to be brave enough to say, "I accept all this responsibility for everything I'm going through. This is what I signed up for as an entrepreneur. This is what I signed up for as a business owner. I don't resent anyone else who is not going through it." This can be hard. It's hard on the nights you've been beaten down by the world, and you're sitting around the table with your family, and you want to collapse. When you're lying in bed and asking yourself, "How am I going to get up and do this again tomorrow?"

Often, at the end of the day, I would walk from my desk to my bed, which was about fifteen feet away, stretch out my arms, and fall back. Lying there with no energy, I'd look over at my wife and do the same double tap I do in jiu jitsu, jokingly telling her that I was tapping out on the day. Almost like clockwork, as soon as I tapped, my phone would ring, and the evening barrage of calls would start. Every night it was a different employee with a different problem. My days were spent battling to keep the business alive, and my nights were spent dealing with people who were at their breaking points. I would remind them they were still alive, and they still had a job, so we were lucky enough to get to do it again tomorrow.

I was not perfect at this by any means. Some nights I was miserable to be near. However, sometimes you have to tap out and say, "I tap tonight. This day got the best of me, but I'm not dead. I'm not giving up. Tomorrow, I'll come back for more," or "I tap out to my base self. I tap out to my ego, and tomorrow I'm going to do better. I'll be of service to my family. I'll be a better brother (or sister or son or husband or wife)."

They may recognize your efforts—or they may not. Recognition and appreciation should not be the reason you try to be better. You should go out and be of service to the people in your life whenever you can. Embody the principle, and good things will follow over time. Have a service mindset to your whole family, all of your friends, and all of your network, no matter what you're going through, what's going on in the world, or whether they're reciprocating or not. If they're important enough to be in your life, you should be of service to them. The good karma you're going to get from being of service to the people in your life should be enough of a reason to do it.

This is especially important in father-in-law and mother-in-law dynamics. It's your job to be of service to them, put your ego aside, and be an incredible son-in-law or daughter-in-law. Accept them for all their flaws and faults. You'll find this will lead you to become a better son or daughter too—if you can get to the point of understanding and empathizing. Most people cannot do this. The advice I'm imparting here is world championship, black belt level. I recognize that it can be hard.

However, it's your job to always have your significant other's back while also promoting a great relationship with their family. Don't be the person who is always trying to rip their significant other away from their family. Your spouse is always going to have conflict with their siblings and parents. You don't want to be the person who marries into the family and then breaks them apart like Yoko Ono.

You want to be the glue. Be the person in your community, network, and family who crosses borders, brings people together, and challenges them to change the way they think. Nurture all your relationships, regardless of the fact that all of them are flawed. Encourage them to call the other person up and apologize. "But you don't understand! They did this. They said that." It doesn't matter. Call them and apologize. You're going to feel better, and they're going to feel better. Nine times out of ten, they'll also apologize.

My sensei often tells us iron sharpens iron. You develop stronger bonds and stronger relationships when you embody this behavior yourself.

Mat Chat

One of the principles in Jocko's book *Extreme Ownership* is called detachment, which refers to being able to detach from a situation. When Navy SEALS are in a firefight, staring down the barrel of a gun, shooting at the enemy, they can have tunnel vision on whatever they're shooting at. In order to make the right decision, you have to detach from the situation, get off your rifle, look around, and then make a decision. Too often, people can get so focused on what's going on down the barrel that they don't take the time to appreciate all the facts and events happening around them, so they make a bad decision and run into a disaster.

The principle of detachment is simple to understand and hard to practice. When you're dealing with the people who are closest to you in your life and they do or say something that hits one of your triggers, you find that you fall back into your base self. Your fuse is short because this thing has happened so many times in your past, and before you know it, you're in a full-blown argument. These don't have to be big triggers. They could be pet peeves.

Sometimes, they're things that were done unintentionally. Sometimes, they're done very intentionally, just to get a rise out of you. You have to learn how to detach from the situation, look around, and realize what the intention is.

For instance, if we're sitting around the dinner table and the topic of a lawsuit comes up, my mom's natural instinct is to tell me to sue them back. Now, she has no experience with lawsuits, so she doesn't know this is bad advice. Her instinct is to protect her children, and she gets mad at people who are "doing something bad." She doesn't understand that like in *A Bronx Tale*, I'm metaphorically spending $20 to get rid of my problem (as we discussed in Chapter 5)—and she probably never will. She is simply jumping into mama bear mode because she sees someone attacking her cub.

My wife likes to remind me, "When the elephants fight, it's the grass that gets trampled." When you're having a fight with your mom at the dinner table, the grass is the kids and your siblings and the family friend.

I've developed my muscles so much that when an employee walks into my office, they can rarely rattle me. I haven't lost my temper with an employee in years. If you're going to be successful in business, you can't chew people out or scream at them. In other words, you can't talk to them the way you talk to your siblings. And if you can't talk that way to your employees and customers, you probably shouldn't talk that way to the people you love the most.

Understand and look at the dynamics within your

own family. No matter how much you try to work on yourself, no matter how good you get at business, and no matter how good you get at jiu jitsu, your family and close friends have a way of bringing you back to your base self faster than anyone else.

The closest people in your life can be your biggest fans, or they can be your greatest obstacles. But the truth is, every single person can be either of those things. They can propel you forward, or they can hold you back. At the end of the day, the only thing you can control is how you react. Whether or not the people around you have your back or are your biggest supporters, your job is to think clearly; make rational, ethical, and moral decisions; and win and succeed despite the noise.

Chapter 7
Networking

We have a saying at my dojo: each one, teach one, reach one. Essentially, this means knowledge was passed on to you from your sensei or someone teaching you, and the only way to propagate it is to pass it on to someone else.

This is in stark contrast to the way many traditional martial arts were practiced in the past. Then, the master or guru would stand at the front and pass knowledge on to their disciples, but it was considered secret knowledge. Those disciples were not allowed to pass it on to anyone else. Today, we take a very different approach. With easy access to social media and YouTube, there are endless instructional videos you can watch and learn from.

Jiu Jitsu Principle: Passing on Knowledge

The essence of my podcast, *Business Jiu Jitsu,* started because over the years, both before and after practice, my jiu jitsu teammates who were interested in business or wanted to start a business would come over and ask me questions. In the locker room, they'd pepper me with how I got started, how I built my website, how I grew a following on social media, how I'd handle a situation they were in, and so on. They had so many different, interesting questions that I had a lot of experience in. So I would explain to them the little truths I had learned, which were usually surprisingly simple.

For example, one of my dojo friends, Jack, was talking to me about wanting to start his business. He mentioned that he didn't know where to start.

Me: The dojo's a great place to start. Do you know Peter?

Jack: Which one's Peter?

Me: Stop. You've been training here for over two years. I've seen you on the mat with Peter over a hundred times. How do you not know who I'm talking about?

Jack: Well, I know his face. Does he have a nickname?

Me: Here's your homework. Every time you walk into the dojo, I want you to walk around to every person in the room, look them in the eye, and shake their hand. Don't stop until you know every single person's first name, last name, and what they do.

It often happens that when you're with the same group of people over and over, people start to get nicknames. "That guy's from Valley Stream, so we're going to call him Valley." People adopt these nicknames, which is fun, but it can keep you from actually getting to know them.

I said to Jack, "These people are your team. They're your network. Peter's a plumber. Rob's in sanitation. Matt's in marketing. This dojo has all the people you could potentially need in your life. At the very least, it's a starting point. If you need a plumber, you can call Peter. If you need help marketing a product, you call Matt. We have schoolteachers, nurses, physical therapists. The mat is made up of a whole world of people."

Then, I turned the tables on him. "How many of them know what you do?" (Jack was a realtor.) I went on, "How many homes have you sold for people in the dojo?"

Jack: None.

Me: I bet they don't even know you're a realtor. You have to make it known.

As we were having this conversation, one of our dojo friends walked over, having overhead. "Dude, you're a realtor? I just listed my house this week! I don't even know the guy I used. I would've given it to you."

Jack looked at me in the way that people get when they figure out that a jiu jitsu technique actually works. He understood what I was saying to him. There was a whole room full of people who needed to buy a house, rent a house, sell a house, lease an apartment, etc. And if not them, their family and friends would. They were his referral source.

These principles seem like they can't be that easy. But they are that easy. They're easy in the way that doing pushups or going for a run is easy. Conceptually, they're easy to learn, but they're hard to practice and make a part of your life every single day.

Your success in business and your success with your network are directly proportional to the habits you make around how actively and seriously you take your network—and the action you take.

Tim Hennessey, owner of C2X Academy, wrestling coach, and high-performing businessman, only became a part of my network because of my instinct to take action. A few years ago, a video of Tim's blew up on TikTok, and when I saw it, I knew I wanted to have him on the podcast.[30] As soon as I had the thought, I took action by messaging him right then. I didn't wait until I had the perfect wording or the perfect time.

After he came on the podcast, we made sure to keep in touch. The next time he was in New York, he called me, and we went out to lunch. That summer his daughter Brynn interned at Mixology. A few months later, we attended a Rutgers wrestling match together. My goal when reaching out to Tim wasn't to add him to my network. I simply wanted to have a great conversation. By virtue of speaking to him

---

[30] Ep. 61: Tim Hennessey | My Podcast Business Plan w/ Tim Hennessey founder of C2X Academy

authentically and from the heart, I was able to build a great friendship with an incredible person. If I hadn't had the muscle memory to take action, I never would have made that connection, and none of the lunches and podcast appearances would have happened.

In order to tap into the power of a network, you first have to recognize you have one. But you also have to be a good member of that network.

Business Principle: Networking

Many business owners expect and count on friends to support their business. I have a different philosophy. I don't expect anyone to support me. If they want to support me, I'm appreciative. If your business relies completely on your friends, you're not going to have a very good business. I have had salespeople who count on their friends to buy every single time they come in as if that's how they prove their love. Those salespeople are in good standing if their friends spend a lot that month. And if they don't? That's how friendships—and jobs—are ruined.

Now imagine how that makes the friends feel. Why would they ever come to support your business? You've probably heard the adage that friends shouldn't do business with friends. I disagree. I think the adage should be reframed: friends shouldn't rely on friends for business.

You don't know what a person is going through. You don't know if they've had a change in their job or if they've hit a rough patch. If they're your friend, you should support them unconditionally. As long as they're a good person, not toxic, and not bringing you down, there's a place for them in your life. You don't need to cut them out because they're not supporting your business.

When you feel disappointed because people aren't supporting you, it's time for you to be of service to them. Especially if they've supported you consistently in the past, it may be a sign that something is going on in their life.

When I'm coaching a teammate, employee, or friend starting a new business, I have them make a list of all the people in their life: friends, family, coaches, teachers, pastors, rabbis, and so on. We look at each name on the list, and instead of asking, "What can they do to help me?" I have the person ask themselves, "What have I done for them lately?" When you start a business, it's natural that you want people to come out of the woodwork and support you.

However, people won't go out of their way to help someone who's selfish. If you're not being of service to the network, the network is not going to be of service to you. A common criticism I hear when talking about networking is that networkers are being fake in order to get things out of others. It's true that this can happen, but I've found the people who are being fake don't get very far because they're always asking, asking, asking.

In 2022, I started a very large, very expensive renovation of my home. It's over a hundred years old, and it has a hundred-year-old boiler that's falling apart and covered in asbestos. I knew when I bought the house that I'd have to do this project. When it came time to pick the contractor, I knew exactly who to call: Ray Mohler, owner of Carefree Air Conditioning in Lynbrook, New York.

Why Ray? In those first terrifying days of COVID, when my dad started making calls to his network, one of his first sales was a $500 gift card order from Ray. You never forget the people who have your back in the dark times. Even though I have over thirty HVAC contractors and vendors all over the country—with five in the New York City metro area alone—I chose Ray. We have a term in Yiddish called a mensch, which means someone who embodies honor, integrity, and trustworthiness—essentially, a great human. Ray is a mensch.

You Do Have a Network

A larger concern I've found new entrepreneurs come up against is they think they don't have a network.

When a friend from my dojo asked me for help with his business, I suggested reaching out to his network.

Friend: I don't have a network.

Me: Then how are you talking to me right now?

Friend: (The lightbulb started to ignite.)

Me: I'm your network. I'm helping you right now. Last week, when you were in my office, didn't my dad pull you aside and talk to you?

Friend: Yeah, he did! That was awesome.

Me: Did you send him a thank-you note?

Friend: No, I didn't think about that.

I told him the next time someone offered him advice or help, he should send them a thank-you note (preferably a physical one if possible, but an electronic one would do if he didn't have or couldn't get their address). It didn't have to be long:

> *Hey Glenn,*
>
> *Thank you so much for taking an interest in me last week. My career's just getting started. I'm really looking forward to doing big things. I hope to keep you in mind. I'll keep you updated on everything I'm doing.*
>
> *Thanks,*
>
> *Friend*

So we start by creating a list of people you know. Sometimes, the next step is emailing this list to inform them about your new business. But if you want to know if that email will be successful, you have to consider what you have done for this group of people. Have you kept in touch with them? Have you sent them Christmas cards? Have you supported their charities? Have you shown up to their birthdays? Have you been of service to them? The answer to those questions is whether you should expect them to support you.

Here's the catch-22: simply because you are being

of service to them does not mean you can expect them to be of service back.

When you send your email out, some people are going to respond, "Congratulations!" Others will support you. Some will ghost you and pretend they've never met you before. And others will send you bad wishes behind your back, not well wishes. That's okay. All you're looking for is a little bit of momentum to get started.

You are practicing your networking skills on the people who support you. You are learning how to build your network from your existing network. Then you have to go out of your way to make sure that they get unbelievable service because network and business, most of the time, come from referrals. "You have to talk to my nephew. He's incredible. He's so consistent." These are the things you want people to say about you. If you are genuinely not those things and are not of service, you will have difficulty building your network.

Even if people don't help you, continue to be of service to them, support them, and be there for them. Let's say you have a landscaping company. They might not give you their business because their brother-in-law is already their landscaper or they've been using a close family friend for twenty years. But if you're in a different territory, and they have a friend or family member who moves into your neighborhood—boom. They're going to tell that person about your business. You never know who could be a great source of referrals, even if they don't support you monetarily.

The "pay it forward" philosophy and being of service have had incredible compounding effects on my life. I've watched other business owners who are spiteful, and it's always about them: "I can't help you unless you help me first." I take a different approach. If someone comes to me and it's within my power to help them, I help them, whether that's giving business advice or monetary support.

Mat Chat

Years ago, one of my longtime investing partners, Ben Zises, came to me with an investment opportunity. The company was called Caraway, and the CEO was Jordan Nathan. At the time, Nathan was about twenty-five years old. He had built a huge network during his time working as a direct-to-consumer e-commerce marketer for a large home goods company, and he was ready to start his own business.

When Nathan approached Ben for investment, he had no startup experience, and because the company was pre-revenue, there was no company to underwrite. Ben grilled Nathan with a million questions, and I'll never forget the reason I invested. While explaining what questions he had asked, Ben said, "I asked him how much he paid in rent. I wanted to know if the kid was a spendthrift."

I immediately stopped him and said, "If that's how deep you went with him and you think he's competent, then I do too."

Caraway has exploded with growth since then, and

Nathan has proven to be an incredible business owner. One of my favorite things he does is send quarterly emails to his investors. While quarterly updates are expected by investors, Nathan's updates are incredibly concise and clear. They contain all the information investors want with no extra fluff, colorful language, or rosy paragraphs.

And at the end of each email, he includes a "how you can help" section, where he details how investors can help grow the company they've invested in. He engages his entire network to support him and his company, whether it's open roles they are looking to fill or a connection he needs.

Whether you're a good member of your academy or of your community, the principles of networking are muscles you need to continue to work just like any other muscle. Your community is an important part of foundation that will help you overcome challenges, and as we talk about in the next chapter, sometimes your greatest challenge is your own inner monologue.

Chapter 8
Internal Competition

We've talked about recovering our guard and finding our offense, along with the importance of muscle memory. You don't rise to the level of your expectations but fall to the level of your training. You've read how I was able to successfully navigate the challenges of COVID because of implementing the technical framework I learned in jiu jitsu to the other areas of my life.

However, remember what we talked about in Chapter 3: don't beat yourself up if you've failed because you're a beginner. If your business failed and you're reading this book because you're trying to dig your way out of it, that's excellent. You're still fighting.

The only way to get better at jiu jitsu is to keep showing up every single night. You'll experience peaks and valleys, injuries and illnesses—things that take you off the mat. But if you keep showing up, you'll keep improving. The techniques turn into instinctive reactions, needing no extra thought—even showing up can become muscle memory.

The Japanese have a concept called *mushin*, which means "mind without mind" or "no mind." (This concept can also be found in Chinese, Zen, and Daoist practices.) The philosophy of mushin is extremely simple—and extremely deep. Mushin means to quiet your inner monologue, to react and act without thinking about each step in a process or what the right decision is.

How do you know you're making the right decision? You can't remember every book you've read, every podcast you've listened to, or every decision you've made in the past. By filtering the framework explained throughout this book through your core values, you can begin the learning process, and eventually, the learnings will become muscle memory.

When you start learning jiu jitsu, you might overthink each move. But here's the thing: if you're busy thinking, your opponent's already making their move. The key is to trust your training and let your reactions flow naturally.

Jiu Jitsu Principle: Quiet Your Mind

Picture this: you're stepping onto the jiu-jitsu mat for the first time, and it's like diving into a vast, unfamiliar ocean where you can't yet gauge its depth. The initial sense of being overwhelmed is undeniable. Yet as weeks turn into months, you find your footing, and a flood of questions surfaces.

Some newcomers ask technical questions, such as "Where should I put my hand?" or "Why is it positioned there?" Meanwhile, others might challenge the very technique they're being taught, exclaiming, "This move doesn't seem effective; I'd rather try this instead." It's crucial to understand the distinction between these two mindsets.

This is where the concept of mushin comes into play. Before you become a master of any craft, it's essential to silence your ego. Every discipline, be it jiu jitsu, boxing, or even the corporate world, has foundational principles. Mastering these fundamentals is why you can later innovate and create your own distinct style.

You wouldn't march into an art class and tell your art teacher, "I don't want to do traditional figure drawing. I want to be abstract like Picasso. I don't need to learn anatomy." If you study Picasso's earlier works, you'll find that he developed his style over years. He didn't begin as a master of abstract art. Many legendary figures served apprenticeships, soaking in knowledge until they could innovate. In his book *The Art of Learning*, Josh Waitzkin calls this "learning form to lose form."

You're learning all these fundamentals to unlearn them later when you create your own style. When first starting in any field, you're like an infant learning the ropes, mastering basics like walking or speaking. And akin to rebellious teenagers, you might begin questioning these very basics: "Why do this? What if you do this? But what if you do this?"

The answer is there's always an answer. "If you do that, I will do something else because I'm better than you." There's wisdom in the foundational techniques.

If you challenge a seasoned practitioner with an alternative technique, they'll counteract swiftly, simply because they've been in the game longer. If I own a chain of pizza shops and you open up a pizza shop next to me, I'm going to do something better than you just by virtue of doing it longer. I know how to plan a schedule. I know how to run a team. I know how to run a successful business. If you've only made pizzas in your home kitchen and opened a shop with grand dreams, good luck catching up with me and my corporate orders. (Of course, it's not impossible.)

One of my closest friends, Sal, owns Joe's Pizza NYC, widely considered to be one of the best slices of pizza in New York City (and the world). People wait in lines around the block at his shops to get a slice. I asked him once what his secret to sustained success was. He said, "Anyone can make one perfect pie. The trick is to make thousands of perfect pies every day for decades."

The path to mastery involves fostering a mindset of openness—which means being able to quiet your mind. Occasionally, when I'm reading a book, a little devil will pop into my head and say, "Well, you do it this way, and that's better," or "No, no, no, we tried that, and it didn't work." In those moments, I have to actively silence this voice, soak in the wisdom, and understand that there's a lesson in every experience— even if it's learning what not to do. As Tony Robbins said, "Success leaves clues." Surround yourself with mentors and positive influence, and the knowledge will follow.[31]

Mushin: No Mind

I'm often asked how to quiet the mind. The most common advice is to meditate, but one of the hardest parts of meditating is quieting your mind. Some meditative practices tell you to focus on your breath, which can work for a few minutes for the untrained, but it's very, very hard to do for an extended period of time.

The way I prefer to quiet my mind is by distracting my mind. I do this through reading physical books and listening to audiobooks and podcasts. But, sometimes when you do this, your mind might not be receptive to the information. This is where awareness comes in. You need to catch yourself in the act, acknowledge you're doing it again (disproving new knowledge), and re-quiet your mind.

Quieting your mind requires you to be honest with your thoughts. Understand which thoughts are productive and which thoughts aren't, when you're judging people and when you aren't, and when you're thinking through things critically.

This applies to your business as well. For example, the first quarter of 2022 was extremely difficult for

---

[31] It's important that you're careful who you're learning from, whether it's jiu jitsu, business, or life advice. There are false gurus, misleading fraudsters, and charlatans. These types of people will do everything possible to get you to follow them down a path that leads to doing bad things—and it's really easy to do them.

Mixology Clothing Company. There was the Ukraine war, hyperinflation, high gas prices, talks of recession, and terrible weather in New York—we lost two full weekends of sales from being closed for snowstorms. Plus, two of my key employees were out with serious family medical issues.

When it was time to analyze Q1 with the executive team, I told them, "I want to be real with this. I don't want to use the weather, missing employees, or any other events as excuses." I had them add back the missed weekends and the stores with the missing employees to the data. We looked at the business with all things being equal and asked ourselves, "Are we making the right decisions? Did we run the right promotions? Is the team clicking? Or do we have to make a radical change?"

Our analysis was an introspective: "Let's not kid ourselves. Let's not make excuses. Let's figure out if we're actually doing a good job or if we're heading into disaster." We called ourselves out. We looked at the things we couldn't control versus the things we could, figured out how to fix the things we could control, and didn't beat ourselves up over the things we couldn't control.

We were able to enter Q2 with a solid understanding of the current state of business, a plan of where we were going to make changes, and a knowledge of where to keep an eye out for potential problems.

In the fall of 2023, I had to recognize that a bad decision was made and stop the team from making another bad decision to cover for it. Anticipating a strong Q3, we purchased a lot of inventory—that ended up sitting in a warehouse because New York City saw intense rain on twenty-one out of twenty-two weekends.

Looking into the problem, I had to ask myself if we had made the wrong buying decisions, if it was bad merchandise, or if the hot, rainy, unseasonable weather was the problem (it was the latter). Then, I had to decide what action to take. My buying team wanted to hold the inventory and reintroduce it next season. I disagreed. A business fundamental is that money should always be compounding. In order for inventory to compound, it needs to turn. It can't do that sitting in boxes.

One of my biggest business influences was my professor at Harvard Business School Online, Mihir Desai. During his class on finance, he talked about the Parable of the Talents, which comes from the New Testament.[32]

Before embarking on a journey, a master allocates his wealth among three of his servants based on their abilities. The first servant receives five talents (a historical currency), while the second is given two, and the last one is entrusted with one. Seeing opportunity, both the first and second servants invest the money wisely and double it. The third servant, out of fear or apprehension, chooses to bury his talent, ensuring no

---

[32] Desai also talks about this concept in his book *Wisdom of Finance*.

gain or loss.

Upon the master's return, he reviews their actions. He praises the first two servants for their initiative and resourcefulness, rewarding them for their efforts. He expresses disappointment with the third servant, highlighting a missed opportunity to even minimally increase the initial amount by depositing it with bankers. The core message? It's imperative to utilize our resources, gifts, and capabilities actively rather than allowing them to sit untouched.

After I told the story to my team, we decided to find a way to get scrappy and move the inventory. It was pointed out that the inventory would be great for our expansion into Florida, but the store wasn't going to open until February. Instead of yet another obstacle, I saw an opportunity.

Rather than waiting for the Florida store to open—when the perfect selling season would be past—I flew down, found a place to open a pop-up store, hired several employees, and flew back, all in a single day. Our inventory was sent down, and the pop-up was ready to open on November 1, less than two weeks from the decision to not hold on to the goods.

The inventory was no longer buried, wasting opportunities. It was invested wisely and compounded our investment. There was a risk it could be a total failure. However, by taking the chance, we had the opportunity to win. By storing the goods, we were guaranteed to stagnate, like the third servant burying the talents.

If you've made a perceived bad decision, don't go

on the defense and make another bad decision to try to cover your first bad decision. It's better to take a risk than accept a guaranteed loss.

When you're looking inside yourself, licking your wounds, and trying to figure out what to do next, you have two options. One, start to create momentum back into a good decision. Two, if you've taken too much risk and made a bad decision because of bad behavior, recognize the problem and correct the behavior.

I see this often in jiu jitsu when someone has a horrible injury and can't train in their typical fashion, so they decide to eat and drink themselves into oblivion instead of refocusing their energy on a new area. You can't run? Focus on upper body strength. Instead of accepting a perceived weakness, focus on an area where you can win.

Think of the common image of the devil and angel on your shoulders. When something bad happens to you, the devil is going to say to you, "You fucked up. You are bad. You made a bad decision. Do something else." You have to ask yourself if it's worth giving up because of one setback. Should you quit jiu jitsu because you got hurt?

For years, a relative would always joke to me that jiu jitsu was too dangerous for Jewish people because we're "learned people." Then, while walking his dog, he fell and broke his shoulder and collarbone. I was finally able to joke back to him, "That's supposed to happen to me in jiu jitsu, not to you while walking your dog!" (Don't worry; I made sure he was going to be okay before I made the joke.)

My point is that anything can happen to anyone at any time. It's not about the decision to practice jiu jitsu or walk your dog. It's about choosing to analyze your own decision-making and the outcomes. Why did you make that decision? What was the outcome? What can you do to mitigate a poor outcome or repeat a good one?

Say you make the decision to open a business. What was the original motivation? Were you well capitalized? Did you build the right team? Did you market yourself appropriately? If the answers are yes but you haven't had the success you're looking for, look for the areas where you need to double down on your work. You might find you're much closer to success than you thought.

Remember in Chapter 3 when I thought I was the biggest loser in the world for trying to build ARC? Although I was tempted, I didn't give up. I quoted my inner monologue, listened to my wife's advice ("When you're ready to give up, you're two millimeters away from success"), analyzed my decisions, found an alternative path, and made it work.

Business Principle: Compete With Yourself First

As we previously discussed, sometimes, after a long day of fighting to keep Mixology Clothing Company open, getting metaphorically beaten up by my family around the dinner table, and knowing my wife was on the front lines in the city, I was ready to give up. When it gets this hard, it's easy to say to yourself, "I wish I wasn't dealing with these problems. I don't want to do this."

This is where the figurative tap comes in. You quiet your mind to go to sleep, knowing you're alive, you're still standing, and you can do this again. Tomorrow, you'll get up, go for a walk, drink a cup of coffee, get on the Zoom call, and inspire your team. You find the little wins, and those are what get you to the next hour, and then the next hour, and then the next hour.

On the *Business Jiu Jitsu* podcast, Gordon Ryan told me a story about fighting Craig Jones in the finals of the EBI tournament.[33] The fight went into overtime, which meant sudden death by either riding time or submission. During overtime, Craig trapped Gordon in the deepest, nastiest armbar I've ever seen. On the podcast, I asked him, "Why didn't you tap?" His reply was remarkable.

"First, I didn't tap because I was undefeated. I had $20,000 riding on the line. But the real reason I didn't tap? It's because I was able to keep moving. In order to finish that armbar, he had to keep me in a static position. Even though my arm was breaking, even though it was stretched to the max, I could move. And because I was able to move, I was able to break out of it."

Being able to move is why I didn't tap to the pressures of COVID. As the days kept creeping (or

---

[33] Ep 20: Gordon Ryan | Being Authentic & Never Giving In

racing, depending on the day), I found some little way to stay alive every single day. I didn't win every day, but I also didn't lose every day. Some days, our sales were amazing; some days, they were mediocre.

Yes, I was in a metaphorical submission that I had to escape, but they couldn't hold me down. They locked me in my house, so I moved to Zoom. They said I couldn't sell in stores, so I sold online. As long as I could keep making decisions, I found new ways to have little wins. So many business owners gave up during COVID because they couldn't handle the pressure or they didn't want the pressure.

I've seen this happen many times in jiu jitsu. You have a big, strong monster on top of you, and you can't breathe. His arm is across your face. He's sweating on you, and the smell, the heat, the blood pulsing in your ears i's all too much. But there's one little thing you can do to make it all stop—you can tap.

There's nothing wrong with tapping to that day or when you're training in practice. But when you're Gordon Ryan, your back's against the mat, your arm's about to break, you have $20,000, and you're undefeated, you don't tap. In EBI overtime rules, you have a set amount of time to submit your opponent. If you submit them, it goes to sudden death rules, and they have one chance to attempt to submit you. If they don't get you to tap, you win. Or your opponent can ride that time out, refuse to tap, and escape. If the time expires, whoever has had the most time pinning the other person wins.

Gordon escaped the submission, rode out his

riding time, and had the chance to submit Craig Jones, which he did—all with a broken arm.

Why didn't I tap out during the pandemic? Because I had enough control of my ego to metaphorically tap at the end of the night and still come back to training every single day. Every single day of COVID was a training session. You can tap a million times in training, but you don't tap to the event, which was surviving 2020–2021. That was the gold medal moment. I won because I kept coming back, day after day.

When asked what the highlight of his fighting career was, Renzo Gracie said it was the moment his elbow was dislocated and the fight was stopped against Kazushi Sakuraba in August 2000:

> In my life, I always believed that if I had an injury, I would never give up. "If that happened in the fight, in the old times, people would keep fighting in the ring. But they stopped the match. In reality, my whole life, I thought I would do that in that situation. I would never tap. But you can never be 100 percent sure until that moment arrives and you feel that pain. That was the most pain I ever felt in my life, but I was happy I went through that, even though it hurt a lot. I was smiling the whole time. It was the moment I found out my mind was stronger than my body.[34]

---

[34] Meltzer, Dave. 2015. "Renzo Gracie Looks Back at Sakuraba Fight." MMA Fighting. March 8, 2015.

One of the defining moments of Renzo's life was a tragic loss because he did what he had always hoped to do. It's a great example of the unbreakable spirit. You might shatter me, but I remain whole. Knock me down, and I'll rise stronger.

Imposter Syndrome

A common concept discussed in business (and in life) is the idea of imposter syndrome. Many people advise you to "fake it 'till you make it." I hate this advice. There's a fine line between faking it and having confidence.

Too many people step into the ring and expect a one-punch knockout. That's exceedingly rare. Conor McGregor, Mike Tyson, Michael Jordan, Tom Brady: these guys are once in a generation. This is not a book for the once-in-a-generation people. This is for regular people who get up every day, go to work, work hard, have a great family, and want to evolve into something that transcends themselves.

It's great to learn from Gordon Ryan, John Danaher, Renzo Gracie, Tony Robbins, and bigger-than-life people. I aspire to be them one day myself. But remember, most of them didn't start as one-punch knockouts either. It's vital to never stop learning. Continue to humble your ego enough to say, "I don't know about marketing." Then read a book, listen to a

https://www.mmafighting.com/2015/3/8/8160649/renzo-gracie-reflects-on-the-sakuraba-fight-and-his-life-changing#:~:text=%22In%20my%20life.

podcast, or take a course about marketing (or do all three), and take action.

If you're humble enough to be upfront and real with the people in your life, whether stakeholders in your business or those closest to you, instead of "faking it," you create some of the longest and greatest relationships in your life.

Here comes the hard part: it takes time.

Getting your black belt in jiu jitsu takes years—usually over a decade. Newcomers often ask how long it takes to get their black belt and are surprised by the answer. "But I got my karate black belt in three and a half years!"

> Coach: Jiu jitsu is a little bit different. Did you wrestle in college?
>
> New student: No.
>
> Coach: What about high school?
>
> New student: No.
>
> Coach: Do you work out every single day?
>
> New student: No.
>
> Coach: Okay. When was the last time you did anything athletic?
>
> New student: Well, I haven't really been training the past few years.
>
> Coach: Then it's probably going to take you ten to fifteen years to earn your black belt—if you're able to earn it at all.

New student: I don't have ten to fifteen years!

Coach: Then maybe the jiu jitsu life isn't for you.

The same conversation can be applied to your business life as well. One of my best friends and college roommate Sam Zises once told me, "It takes ten years to make an overnight success." The people who come out of college faking it are not as impressive as the ones who are grinding, asking great questions, showing up every day to learn, taking risks, and trying to grow.

The "fake it till they make it" people tend to end up as documentaries on Netflix, such as Billy McFarland with the Fyre Festival fiasco; Martin Shkreli, who bought patents on lifesaving drugs and then increased the prices; Anna Delvey, who pretended to be a fake German heiress; Elizabeth Holmes, who created and sold a blood testing device that didn't work; and, most recently, Sam Bankman Fried (SBF) who committed fraud using his cryptocurrency exchange FTX and trading firm Alameda Research.

In all five of these cases, the problem was not that they weren't smart, talented, or unconnected. They were all larger than life and looked unstoppable. They all had celebrity endorsements and connections with millionaires, billionaires, high-level military, and investors. What they didn't have was honesty and integrity. They lived by the mantra "fake it 'till you make it."

Now, some people do manage to make it while faking it—but once they're exposed, they always crumble. The one time I tried to fake it was when I went into Keith Miller's office filled with bravado and early success. Once he started quizzing me and I didn't have the answers, I was quickly exposed as a white belt. I never made that mistake again.

Everyone will have a moment when you have to make a business decision that could win you the deal, and you either have the goods or you don't. You have the opportunity to be upfront with your customer or lie to your customer. The best businesses in the world always choose to be upfront.

A great example of being upfront is my business partner, Arya Sajedi, who you met in Chapter 3. When I hired Arya, I knew he was different immediately. Usually, consultants want to be paid upfront and have you sign a six-month minimum contract. Arya did not. He asked for one month's pay before I signed any long-term contracts or paid any deposits. He wanted to get to know the company, the problem, and the desired solution before he wrote his proposal. It was the opposite of faking it 'till you make it. He told me exactly what he was going to do and how he was going to do it. It made for an incredible foundation for our relationship.

Too many people have a toxic business (and life) philosophy of "you have to fuck them before they fuck you."[35] You see this philosophy with a lot of people (too many people). They're bragging about being an

---

[35] Someone said this exact quote to my father—while putting his feet up on Dad's desk.

asshole. The worst part is they don't even realize they're being the bad guy. Everyone thinks they're the good guy in their own story.

This voice inside your head can be your biggest friend or your biggest obstacle. It's the angel and the devil on your shoulders, and they're talking to you all day, every day.

It's up to you to quiet your mind and ask yourself, "I think I'm making the right decision here, but why am I making this decision?" or "I made that decision, and it didn't work out. Is there something I need to keep doing, or do I need to make a change?" These are hard moments.

Mat Chat

It's common to think of the opponent or the other business when you think of competition.

Many people are surprised to find that I have never been a competitive person. I played sports when I was younger, but I didn't care if we won or lost. Even when I was playing lacrosse and skiing at Northeastern University, I didn't love being in the moment of the big game when everything was riding on me and the coach was yelling. I loved the sport itself, learning strategy, and connecting with the team.

Even today in business, I don't focus on my competitors. I focus on who is doing it best in the world. I don't care what some other operation on Long Island is doing. I want to know how Chanel is doing it. In other words, my biggest competition has always been myself. If I can be better than I was, that's good enough for me.

When I was growing up, I was considered an average student and an average athlete. I was surrounded by incredibly smart and talented people, like my best friends Scott, who played Division 1 lacrosse in one of the best programs in the country; Adam, who played lacrosse at Harvard; Sanford who went to Penn; and Corey, who went to Amherst College. However, unlike them, I always had a job. Their parents wanted them to focus on school and their sports. In my house, the conversation was always around how you were making money.

As a result, my competition centered around how much money I could make. When my friends were going to lacrosse camps and getting SAT tutoring, I was making money caddying—and loving it. Making money lit my fire. During this formative time, I developed a love of working hard and waking up early.

But I didn't feel competition with other people, and I certainly didn't feel competition with my friends. In fact, I couldn't compete with them in many ways. They were Division 1 athletes. They went to Ivy League schools. They accepted jobs with some of the best companies in the world. The only place they couldn't compete with me was in part-time job work experience. Their parents took care of them through college. In fact, the first job most of them had was when they graduated from college. And while most of them are very successful in their jobs, very few of them have become entrepreneurs.

I didn't have to compete directly with them

because I was competing with myself. My father was the same way.

When my dad graduated from college, he went to work for his family's business: delivering housekeepers by van. He would sell people on cleaning their house, pick up the housekeeper, drop the housekeeper off at the house, and then pick the housekeeper up again in the afternoon. It wasn't exactly glamorous.

He was working in an office ten feet wide that barely fit him, his father, and the four administrative employees—the entirety of the company. It was the early 1980s. His friends all went to work on Wall Street. They wore $5,000 suits, bought Rolexes and mansions, and drove Rolls Royces. They were making millions of dollars in their early twenties.

Dad didn't care. He didn't think about what they were doing. Every day, he would wake up and sell, sell, sell. Every year, he kept building the business. He knew if he could compete with himself, he would build something incredible—and he did.

When we started Mixology, it was a single store on Long Island. That's not the most exciting thing for a man in his midtwenties who didn't know or care about fashion. All these years later, it looks incredible. But it didn't start that way. There were no departments or teams. There were no trucks, delivery routes, warehouses, or consultants. There was a small group of mostly women who wanted to be in the fashion business.

It's easy to get in your head and believe you have to

compete with every other store in the community. The company would want to run a sale because the store down the street was running a 20 percent off sale, and they worried if they didn't compete, they'd lose customers. I would say, "Don't look at what they're doing. Look at yourself. Is the store immaculate? How do you treat the customer? Is the inventory treated like gold? Only focus on the things we can control."

Competing with yourself means constantly turning inward, focusing on yourself and what you can do better. It doesn't matter what your friends, your family, or the competition are doing. The biggest competition you have is the things you can control.

In jiu jitsu, business, and life, you have a mix of attributes that are specific to you. If you use your attributes the best way possible, you can always compete. Simply remember you don't have to compete with your direct competitors. Don't look at what they're doing and try to do the exact same thing better. Apple didn't try to recreate the BlackBerry with the first iPhone.

Back then, the BlackBerry was the most popular phone in the world with the biggest market share. They seemed unstoppable. The other big names in the phone industry—PalmPilot, Motorola, and Nokia— were all trying to create the same phone. If you lined all four of those phones in a row, they looked like clones of each other.

Steve Jobs didn't even attempt to compete with them. He took a completely different approach. Instead of focusing on the businessperson who was trying to be productive, he focused on the artists and musicians. He positioned Apple as a champion of the power of the individual against the status quo.

Never focus on what your friends, teammates, or competitors are doing. My sensei reminds us of this often, especially when competitions are coming up. When you show up to a competition, you're going to fight in your belt and weight division. If you're a blue belt, you'll be facing other blue belts of the same weight. You are facing the closest, purest version of yourself.

If you've only been training with people who are much lighter and younger than you and you're used to easily beating them, get ready to come face to face with a rude awakening. In class, it's incumbent upon you to train with as many different types of bodies, sizes, and ages as possible so you can learn how to deal with all those different energies: young people who are fast with a big gas tank, heavy people who can hold you down, older people who are slow but methodical. Every single type of person you train with will help you get ready to face you.

At the highest levels, you can start to focus on external competition, which is what the next chapter is about. Nike versus Adidas. Microsoft versus Apple. But before you can get to the external, you need to make sure the inside is a fortress (the Stoics referred to this as your inner citadel). People can see through the fluff. If you're trying to compete and punch above your weight class, you're going to be found out and defeated fast. But if you've got the goods internally? That's when the fun starts.

Chapter 9
External Competition

"Create dilemmas: Devise maneuvers that give them a choice of ways to respond—all of them bad."[36]

On October 2, 2020, Gordon Ryan competed in a match against Matheus Diniz, who, like Gordon, was a reigning ADCC champion. They both came to the match with impressive win streaks. It was one of the most anticipated matches of 2020, but once it started, the crowd was blown away. Gordon quickly made it look like they were on an uneven playing field and easily dominated Matheus, winning the match with a heel hook. How was he able to defeat such an imposing opponent?

Gordon Ryan talked on the podcast about the importance of creating dilemmas.[37] He explained you want to put your opponent in a position where no

---

[36] Robert Greene, *33 Strategies of War.* New York: Penguin Group, 2006.

[37] Ep 20: Gordon Ryan | Being Authentic & Never Giving In

matter what they do, they fail. When Gordon goes on the mat to compete, he employs a calculated algorithmic approach to jiu jitsu. He thinks through the reactions he'll provoke with his actions. "If I employ this technique, it will evoke this response."

If you are attacking the upper part of the body—head or arms—they will defend those arms, leaving their legs open. When you attack the legs, they'll overcompensate to defend the legs, leaving the arms and neck open, which is where you want to attack in the first place.

The goal is to put your opponent in a position where they must choose the lesser of two evils. By creating dilemmas, you put yourself in a position where you win no matter what happens.

Jiu Jitsu Principle: Creating Dilemmas

As we've broken down over the course of this book, when you begin learning jiu jitsu, you're breaking down techniques into their base parts, like individual musical notes. Then, as you understand these movements, you can start to understand how they connect. Over time, these techniques turn into muscle memory. That's when strategy can start to come into play.

Once you have muscle memory, you start to understand there's an aspect of trickery or tactical awareness. It's not about who's the fastest, the strongest, the one with better technique, or the one who has been training longer. It's often a matter of who has a better game plan or understands the rules better.

Think of this in terms of poker. You can play the cards, or you can play the opponent sitting across from you. The best poker players learn how to play the opponent by focusing on their subconscious tells.

How do you beat the person sitting across from you? Whether it's a battlefield, game table, or mat, the goal is to learn everything you can about your opponent: what their family life is like, what they like to eat, what sets off their temper, what gets them excited, etc. This knowledge helps you understand how you're going to defeat them. If they're quick to anger, make them angry so they lose focus. If they're slow, go fast, and if they're fast, go slow—either way will throw them off their rhythm. You want to be able to set up your attacks with deception, which will increase your odds of causing them a dilemma.

Business Principle: Negotiating Tactics

Creating dilemmas is an important part of negotiating as well. Often, when people don't make a deal they want, they spout off every excuse in the book. Instead of hiding behind excuses, you need to figure out a way to get deals (or transactions, investments, big hires, acquisitions, etc.) made in spite of every obstacle, whether that's price or terms or if they're a jerk or they're nice.

Every single negotiation for every single business deal has a different story. No matter if you're negotiating a contract or lease or buying a car at a dealership, your ability to understand what's going on will be dictated by how well you know the rules, your opponent, and your opponent's motivations.

Having great business relationships with people is core to winning over a long period of time. However, it's important to note that the way I approach creating business relationships is not the only way to do it. Some people who have been unbelievably successful and are wealthy beyond your wildest dreams have an approach that is the complete opposite of mine. You have to find the approach that works best for you.

I've found that if you create a network of people you trust and learn how pricing works by educating yourself on the different aspects of your specific industry, you don't have to worry about being taken advantage of. You'll be able to approach every meeting with a positive mindset.

In my case, I operate retail stores and commercial real estate, so it's incumbent on me to understand the cost of labor, building materials, and trades such as HVAC, plumbing, and electric. Does that mean I need to be an expert in all those things? No, but it does mean that I need to have a fundamental understanding of what those things cost so I know what a good price is versus a bad price.

More important than getting the lowest price, however, is to find the person you can work with over and over again because they're reliable and honest. You don't want to sign a contract with someone because they're the lowest price and find, six months later, the job still isn't complete. Trying to save a few dollars ends up costing you a lot more.

I've also found that the people you develop great relationships with will often go out of their way to help you.

One of my first business trips for Mixology Clothing Company was across the country to Los Angeles to visit several of our vendors. One such vendor we had a great relationship with, and he invited us to tour his warehouse while we were there. It was my first time visiting a fashion warehouse.

When we arrived, we saw over twenty workers unpacking boxes that had just arrived from the docks. As they unpacked each box, they scanned the items and then packed those items to ship out to their wholesale customers. Who do you think will be the first to get these newly arrived goods? Is it the customer who hasn't paid their bills from last month, or the customer who negotiated every penny and demanded free shipping? Of course not. At the end of the day, the one who gets shipped the first box of goods is the one who has the best relationship with them, who pays their bills on time, and who understands they also need to make a profit. I knew, watching those workers, that I needed to do my best to be the first box out of the door.

There's a business reason for treating people with integrity, kindness, and respect. However, this isn't to say you should let yourself be taken advantage of or overpay. You still have to hold people accountable, but you can do so while being a kind person.

I approach all my business dealings this way—even

when it comes to my bankers and landlords. Both of these professions have a very poor reputation, typically because they've lost a lot of the public's trust. Landlords, in particular, have always had a bad reputation with most of the public.

But long before I was in the clothing business, I was a landlord, so today I know what it is to be a good landlord and to be a good tenant. When disaster hits, like it did with COVID, you want to know that your landlord's in your corner. If every single check for the past thirteen years has been paid on time, now that you need them to do a favor for you, they'll be more willing to do it because you're a business they want to back.

When I had to call my landlords at the start of the COVID shutdown to tell them I wasn't going to be able to make payments, virtually all of them had the same response: "We're in this together. Pay me when you can pay me." I'm confident that a large part of their reassurance came from the fact that, in the twelve years I had been in business, I had never missed a single rent payment. And then I called the landlord of our Livingston, New Jersey, location. His response? "The rent is due."

Throughout all of COVID, he never changed his tune. It's very easy to lose your temper with someone as unyielding as this. You want to scream and yell and tell them how terrible and unreasonable they are. Instead, I absorbed his energy. I was able to put myself in his shoes, understand what he was going through, and keep the relationship going.

Mixology is still a tenant there, but that was the very

last store we reopened. The landlords who had my back the most were the ones I wanted to pay back first and help bring foot traffic to their properties by reopening. You have to decide who the first check is to and who the hundredth check is to. By being stubborn and inflexible, he became our last priority.

There's a concept in negotiation called "your price, my terms, not both." The essence of this concept is that if you want your price, then you're going to have to live with their terms. Which is more important to you?

Think of a lease for a retail store or office. Business leases can be anywhere from thirty-five pages to over a hundred pages. Every single one of these pages covers terms that may be mutually beneficial, good for one party, or good for the other party. And over the years, that lease gets longer and longer. Most small businesses hyper-focus on the dollar amount they'll pay for rent every month, usually found on page two. But what about pages three through fifty?

The better you understand a lease, the more favorable a deal you can negotiate for yourself, meaning a better deal on rent as well as being able to put more terms on the landlord. Remember, it's your price, my terms, not both. Do you care more about the number on page two or the terms laid out on pages three through fifty?

However, you can use the concept of creating dilemmas to improve your negotiation tactics. When I'm looking for a new lease, I'm extremely cognizant that I need to get my price and my terms. Usually, when you're a smaller or newer business, it's hard to get your price or your terms. But as you grow in status, you'll find others have to take your price and your terms in order to get your business.

When we started Mixology Clothing Company, we were a price taker and term taker because we were small and new. Some of you reading this book who have a new business or are trying to start a business are going to have to be price and term takers at first. You can begin utilizing and leveraging dilemmas in order to get what you want by being aware of them, learning and understanding the subject or situation, and taking the time to get better and better.

As my business grew from one store to three to five to ten, the leases I was able to write became more favorable to me for both price and terms because I had created a proven track record. Today, if a landlord wants to do business with Mixology, I present them with several nonnegotiables on day one.

The first is that we only give a business guarantee, meaning that neither my family nor I personally guarantees the lease. Especially with newer businesses that have no assets, credibility, or track record, landlords want you to personally guarantee that you will pay if your business cannot. If you don't have net worth, they'll ask about your parents, siblings, uncles, aunts, etc. They want to get someone on the hook for the money so they don't get taken advantage of. As your business gains a track record, landlords are more willing to put this term aside.

There are other terms to consider too. Who pays for maintenance? Who's responsible for snow plowing?

Who's responsible for electricity? There's a whole laundry list of terms that need to be negotiated. Your past track record will play a big role in how much negotiation power you have. Some landlords ask for references from your bankers, vendors, and insurance company to find out if you pay your bills on time and if you have a good reputation in your industry.

If your accounts are in good standing and you've developed great relationships, you'll be able to get your top five vendors to write letters of recommendation on your behalf. Instead of considering these people (vendors, insurance companies, bankers) your opponents, consider them your greatest advocates and stakeholders in your business.

It's important to remember that you don't get to choose who the other side of a deal is. If you want to buy a building, you don't get to decide who owns the building you want. If you want to lease a space because it's in the right market with the right tenant mix and the right demographics, you don't get to decide who the landlord is. Sometimes the person on the other side of the table is nasty, rude, racist, or all of the above. But that's not the reason you shouldn't make a deal. If you want to make the deal, then you have to figure out a way to get the deal done.

This is why top executives make so much money. Does Jeff Bezos deserve to be so rich? Does Elon Musk? They make billions because they are relentless at creating opportunities for themselves and their companies. Sometimes they're ruthless, yes, but more often than not, they have to take a win-win approach in order to secure deals and long-term relationships. If you're a wrecking ball of destruction, you gain a reputation, and no one will want to do business with you.

Everyone has their own style. In the military, every branch—Air Force, Marines, Army, Navy—has a different specialty that will help them win in their special circumstances on special terrain and special weather. But they all have the same goal: to win.

Your job is to win. If you want to be successful, you have to figure out a way to win no matter the obstacles. Let's wrap these principles together in the Mat Chat.

Mat Chat

It's extremely important, especially for those who want to be the best in the world, to understand how to be aggressive and how to go after what you want. When you compete, you're going to create enemies. Plus, there's only room for so many people at the top. Nike and Adidas are in a fierce battle for the top spot, and they haven't left room for Under Armour or Puma. That's not to say they can't grow great businesses, but they likely won't make it to top-dog status.

In the last chapter, I explained that my default mode when growing up was to compete with myself. However, when I started training in jiu jitsu, I gained a whole new appreciation for athletic competition, especially when "mano a mano." I was never the best athlete as a kid, but by learning the techniques and practicing until they became muscle memory, I am now able to compete with—and beat—people who are far superior to me athletically.

In Brazilian jiu jitsu, the *kazushi* principle emphasizes the art of off-balancing an opponent, revealing that victory often hinges not on brute strength but on the strategic destabilization of an adversary's foundation. Similarly, in the business world, applying the kazushi principle means leveraging ingenuity and strategic positioning to outmaneuver larger, more established competitors, proving that success is not solely determined by size, speed, or resources but by the ability to creatively disrupt the status quo.

This is one of the many things I love about jiu jitsu. I'm not as fast as other people, and I'm not nearly as strong as them, but I am a little bit tactically smarter. I understand strategy a little bit better.

The kazushi concept and the dilemma concept helped me understand athletic competition and business competition in a whole new way. External competition is not naturally intuitive to me, so I had to go out and learn how to harness it. Similar to learning techniques in jiu jitsu, I learned the concepts of competition over years of refining and refining and refining again. My competitiveness is a learned trait.

I find it interesting that of my friends who were naturally talented at competition from a very young age because they were so fast or strong, most of them don't compete in sports anymore. Some of the smartest people I knew as kids have blown up their careers. Your natural habits can work for you, but they're not the only thing that works for you. When it comes to competition, the biggest factor is how much you're willing to learn and study the concepts of competition.

As I've mentioned several times in this book (because it's important), reading has been my greatest source of information on every topic I've needed to learn. One of my favorite books about external competition is *Grant* by Ron Chernow, recommended to me by Rich Byrne[38], about Ulysses S. Grant. Grant embodies everything we've talked about in this chapter. He was undersized, considered absent-minded, and an introvert. He didn't get into the best schools. His father, who was known to be a bit of a scoundrel, had to help Grant to get to where he wanted to be.[39]

But through the course of a life of learning and growth, he found that what came naturally to him was his understanding of strategy as it related to the art of war. He became a phenomenal battlefield commander who understood the concept of creating dilemmas, how to learn about his opponents, and how to beat his opponents. He was also able to relate to his troops

---

[38] When Rich and I became friends, we started passing book recommendations back and forth. After he was on my podcast, I sent a few of my favorite books to his office. In return, he started sending me some of his favorite books. This was a natural instinct for me. It was until much later that I realized how many friendships are built (and can be built) on this framework.

[39] Ron Chernow, *Grant*. New York: Penguin Press, 2017.

incredibly well.

Fighting wars is bureaucratic and political. There are political generals who stay out of the actual fray in order to look at the big picture, and there are battlefield generals who are on the field handling the fighting in real time. Grant was one of the most famous battlefield commanders who rose up through the ranks. What made him incredible was his propensity to take risks and lean into his attributes in order to seize the opportunity to win.

Many of his fiercest competitors were generals on his own side who were fighting the bureaucratic war for fame and notoriety. They cared about winning battles, yes, but they also cared about their image. Grant was known for being a mess. He was constantly covered in dirt and grime, and his beard was never maintained. He was always on the front lines with his men, sleeping among the troops, instead of trying to direct from behind the lines based on secondhand reports. An attribute his peers looked down on meant he was able to make the best decisions and seize opportunities that would have been lost if he hadn't been in the fray.

Yet with all that learning, knowledge, and skills, and although he eventually became the eighteenth US president, he died penniless.

I hope this book teaches you how the principles in one area of your life can help you in another area—i.e., how what I've learned in jiu jitsu has helped me in business and vice versa. I think it's incredible that some people dedicate their entire lives to a single purpose, such as winning an Olympic medal, at the sacrifice of everything else. That's not what this book is about.

Instead, I want you to learn from successful people about how to have success in all areas of your life. When you come up against competitors, understand who you're competing against, when you're competing against them, how to make them your allies, and how to make them your stakeholders. There's something to be gained from almost everyone until you get into the highest of the highest levels of competition.

Part Three

Chapter 10
Risk

The first time I trained directly under John Danaher was at the Renzo Gracie headquarters in New York City. During the seminar, he told us a story that has stuck with me.[40]

While coaching mixed martial arts, John had a chance encounter with one of his heroes: boxing legend Bernard Hopkins. During their conversation, they discussed the need to take risks when fighting. Bernard explained to John that fighters are most vulnerable when going on the offensive because while you're attacking, you must let your defenses down, becoming open to counterattack. For example, when you extend your arm to throw a punch, your whole body becomes open.

If you want to win a fight, you eventually have to take the risk of leaving yourself vulnerable. In professional fights when the everything is on the line, fighters tend to dance around each other. Neither

---

[40] Ep. 22: John Danaher | "Language is a Superpower"

combatant wants to commit; they throw half punches and half kicks. They hesitate to take a risk because they know that at the highest levels, even the smallest opening or mistake can be exploited. If you perceive yourself to be even the smallest bit less dominant than the other person, everything can be taken away from you in a moment.

Think about storming a castle. You have to expose your forces to get over the walls while the opponent is behind the wall firing at you. As the attacker, you have the flexibility of movement while they're locked in position. You're the most vulnerable when you feel the most confident: going on the attack.

In both life and in business, taking risks makes you vulnerable—but you can't win without taking risks. If you see a pretty girl across the bar and you don't pluck up the courage to go talk to her, she's never going to agree to a date. This opens you up to rejection, which of course no one wants to feel. No one wants to be rejected, get laughed at, or feel embarrassed by failure.

The concept of opening yourself up to risk is something everyone intuitively understands and experiences on a daily basis. The hard part is understanding the asymmetries of risk. An asymmetric risk is when you want to limit your downside while still maintaining an unlimited potential upside.

Personally, I am not, and have never been, a natural risk taker. My oldest son is like me: cautious, measured, and particular. My youngest son is a wrecking ball with seemingly no fear. Everyone is born with their own natural risk tolerance.

One of my favorite things about jiu jitsu is how much it's taught me about risk. More specifically, it's taught me how to do two things. First is how to take risks commensurate in proportion to my desired outcome. Second is how to ensure that when I do take a risk, I don't end up in a position to lose even if I don't achieve my desired outcome. Ultimately, that's the goal you want to achieve in risk-taking.

Jiu Jitsu Principle: Accepting Vulnerability in Risk

In his book *Breathe: A Life in Flow,* Rickson Gracie discusses a concept he calls "invisible jiu jitsu," which refers to subtle, highly effective techniques that are not immediately obvious. They're not perceived by the casual observer; rather, they're only felt by the fighters.[41] When watching a grappling exchange, people on the outside often ask, "Why don't they just stand up?" They don't understand that when someone more experienced is imposing their will upon you, you can't get up. It feels like there's a wet, heavy blanket on top of you, suffocating you, and no matter what you do or where you move, you cannot throw it off.

John Danaher says that jiu jitsu is a hierarchy of positions that lead to submission. Say you're standing in front of your opponent while they're on their back in

---

[41] Rickson Gracie with Peter Maguire, *Breathe: A Life in Flow.* New York: Dey St., 2021.

the supine position, legs and hands up. You need to get past their dangerous legs—which could kick you in the face or stomach—pin them, control them, and move toward a submission.

The movement, the risk, to try to pass their guard is the moment Bernard talked about earlier. You've exerted most of your energy to get past their legs and pin them down—i.e., attacking the castle. They've used almost no energy because their defenses (gate) are up, so as you move in for the submission, they escape. Because you've exhausted all your energy on your attack, it's easy for them to sweep and turn the tables. You find yourself on your back in a defensive position while they're attacking—except now you're exhausted, and they're looking down at you with a smile on their face. You've walked into a trap.

In competitive situations, it's crucial to balance your resources strategically. Imagine driving from New York to Boston with just enough fuel for the journey. Traveling at sixty-eight miles per hour would be too fast, causing you to run out of gas before reaching your destination. On the other hand, if you maintain a speed of sixty miles per hour, you'll arrive, but you'll be behind schedule. The optimal strategy is to travel at a steady sixty-five miles per hour, ensuring timely arrival without exhausting your resources.

Timing your trip so you get to where you need to go exactly on time with exactly no gas left is the risk mitigation of decision making. You have limited resources and limited time when fighting a match, and the only way you'll win is with an understanding of the fundamentals and your own energy expenditure.

Business Principle: Risk to Succeed

Hedge funds exemplify the concept of measured risk-taking. Unlike traditional banking institutions, they often embrace higher risks. However, they employ strategic hedging to balance these risks. For instance, if a hedge fund invests in a stock anticipating its value will rise (going long), it simultaneously invests in another stock betting its value will fall (short selling). This approach caps potential gains but crucially limits losses too. By balancing long and short positions, hedge funds aim to outperform the market average. They seek a superior return rate, known as "alpha," as opposed to the typical market return, termed "beta."

The decisions I had to make for Mixology Clothing Company during quarantine were unbelievably risky. Some businesses were so afraid that they refused to take any risks—they made decisions that would improve their short-term circumstances but harm them in the long term.

During the COVID-19 pandemic, numerous businesses, paralyzed by uncertainty and fear, made premature decisions that had long-lasting impacts. Examples of such hasty actions were abundant. Many businesses surrendered their leases and shut down, assuming they couldn't sustain through the prolonged quarantine. Others canceled incoming orders for future months like June, July, August, and September without waiting to assess how the situation might evolve. Additionally, a significant number of employers terminated their staff, facing immediate financial constraints, and unfortunately, many failed to maintain communication with these employees for potential rehiring in the future. These decisions, often made in a state of panic, reflected a reluctance to navigate through uncertainty and an inability to strategize for the long term.

These businesses were overly cautious and overly defensive. They made decisions out of fear and were scared to make or commit to decisions. They either did nothing, or worse, they hit the brakes hard and backpedaled. These people thought they were making the right move by being overly defensive.

I took the opposite approach. I knew (and prayed) that the quarantine would eventually end, and when it did, I wanted to be able to hit the ground running. I needed staff to work in the stores. I needed inventory to be able to sell. Every time I had to make a decision, I asked myself what effect the outcome of that decision would have when the government did allow us to reopen. Two of my riskier decisions stand out the most.

Hiring Despite Expense

The first was my decision to honor a job offer I had made to a woman named Jenn Sperber. The second decision I made that stands out was not only not closing stores but opening three stores during and on the heels of COVID.

Right before COVID descended on us, I had offered a job to Jenn. She had been in the fashion business for more than twenty years and was highly recommended by one of my top employees. Jenn had left her old company for two reasons: one, she had moved and was now located near the Hamptons, and two, she had gone on maternity leave. Returning to her company after the move during maternity leave was not an option for Jenn.

After my discussion with Jenn, I presented her with the opportunity to manage the Westhampton Beach location. Traditionally, this store had operated seasonally, opening its doors from May through September. Despite its limited operating months, we incurred year-round expenses, such as rent, taxes, insurance, and landscaping, akin to a full-time store. Historically, the summer revenue was sufficient to cover these annual costs. However, I saw significant potential in the store under Jenn's leadership to transition it into a year-round operation. My rationale was straightforward: if the store's performance during the five-month summer period could justify its annual expenses, then any additional sales generated during the off-season would be a substantial bonus.

That said, the manager would need to be the exact right type of person for this to work. Performing all year at a store that normally closes down is a lot of pressure. It's as if you're running two separate businesses: in the summer season, you have to staff up to handle the high volume, opening the store early and keeping it open late. Then, the summer residents and visitors leave. In order to stay open, you have to completely change your mindset to be a community-driven store that's integrated with the year-round residents and schools. Let me stress just how difficult this opportunity is: it's like being an Olympic wrestler and a Brazilian jiu jitsu black belt simultaneously despite the fact they use different skills and have different rules.

Jenn seemed to be the right type of person. She would be an expensive hire due to her experience and sterling reputation, but I felt confident she would provide a return on the investment and offered her the job with a start date of May 15. Then, COVID hit us like a freight train, and I furloughed one hundred seventy workers. In the early days, I didn't hear from her, which wasn't surprising. In early April, she called me and asked, "Do I still have a job?"

There were two possible answers I could give. The first: "No, I'm really sorry. With the world as it is right now, I can't commit to you." This would have been a perfectly legitimate response. All of my stores were closed, and I didn't know when they would be allowed to reopen. I owed millions in rent, expenses, inventory, etc. The only money going out was to the thirty employees I had kept on to run the business.

Every bone in my body wanted to say no, that I couldn't commit to her right then, but maybe once the world opened back up, we could reevaluate. But something held me back. Instead, I considered the asymmetric risk in this decision. I told myself that if the business was going down, adding one more employee wasn't going to be the reason.

I made a split-second decision based on muscle

memory, years of jiu jitsu, hundreds of books read, dozens of classes taken, and years of business battlefield experience.

Pacing the floor in my dad's office in his Hamptons house, I said, "Jenn, come work for me. I don't know what's going to happen next with COVID, but your start date is still your start date." I took the risk on her, gambling that the government wasn't going to keep us closed forever. And it didn't.

We reopened the Hampton store in June under Jenn's leadership, and she turned out to be one of the best hires I have ever made in my business career. Not only did she significantly grow the business during the summer season, but she also built an unbelievable business during the off-season. **She did exactly what she said she was going to do.**

Making any hire as a small business is hard. It's especially difficult when you're trying to reconcile the fact that your business doesn't have the immediate cash to be able to pay someone outside of the typical pay bracket. This moment of risk is also a moment of faith. Will you take the shot? There's always the chance the hire won't work out and you'll lose money. You may have to take a smaller salary yourself for a while. But as my wife always asks me: what if it does work out?

What if they're the right person? How much will they benefit the business? What's the best-case outcome? Every business that's ever grown to become more than the sum of its parts has experienced this moment of risk and faith. I've been blessed to have had this moment many times—but not every hire has worked out.

She could have been the wrong person. It could have taken me a year of paying her 20–30 percent more than standard to figure out she was the wrong fit. But I wouldn't have known for sure unless I took the risk.

Opening Stores during a Pandemic

The second risky decision I made was to open three stores during and on the heels of COVID. When COVID arrived, we had a store in Roslyn, New York, under construction. It would be our newest store, located in a very affluent market that we had been waiting years to break into. I had to court and beg the landlord, Adam Mann, to land a spot in this brand-new shopping center. It took every ounce of business acumen I had to sell Mixology to Adam, and it worked.

This community is a tight market: there are few vacancies, and rent is extremely expensive. But I knew a store here would be immensely successful if I did everything right. Then, COVID hit. Conventional wisdom would say to pull back, don't spend money, don't open that store. I was temporarily closing all my other stores; why keep building this one?

However, I looked around and saw that despite the impacts of COVID, this particular market was still booming. I decided to stay committed to the store. So when Adam called to ask if we were still going to open, I said, "We're still committed to opening the store. We're going to continue to build." That was the first store.

The second store I decided to take a risk on opening during COVID was a second store in the Hamptons—directly across the street from the current store. Westhampton Beach was overrun with people who, like my siblings and me, had fled New York City. I was seeing lines at the grocery stores, gas stations, delis, and bagel stores. Where other entrepreneurs were thinking defensively and pulling back on their spending, I was thinking about opportunities. Several stores in the Hamptons had closed permanently, leaving vacancies on popular streets. I started considering if we should be opening a second Mixology store.

When I brought the idea up to my team, they thought I had lost my mind. Remember the mood of quarantine: the news was telling us the world was ending. People were locked in their houses. Every time people opened their doors, they put on masks and gloves. Everyone was terrified they would bring home a deadly disease because they had to buy groceries.

Yet during all this fear and trepidation, with all my stores shut down, I was starting a conversation about opening a second store in Westhampton Beach, an area where our singular store was usually seasonal only. My team thought I was insane, and objectively, I could see where they were coming from.

At this point, it was June, so our summer season—when we historically made the most money—was half over, but our revenue wasn't meeting projections. And although some employees who had been furloughed for three months were begging to come back, another whole cohort didn't want to return either due to fear, or because they were happy collecting unemployment and stimulus checks sitting at home.

So while my sister was sick with grief from her wedding being canceled, my executives were terrified: they all thought opening new stores was ridiculous, let alone opening one across the street from an existing location. The only person who didn't think I was crazy was my dad. My dad has a way of looking at every situation as an opportunity. (This was frustrating when I was growing up, but once I started running my own businesses, I realized he was right.)

Unlike the rest of my team, I was looking at the situation as an entrepreneur.

Looking around at this time (around June 2020), I was seeing a lot of pent-up consumer demand. People wanted to shop, and their only option at the time was to order online. Our online business grew over 400 percent during quarantine. We were selling ridiculous amounts of comfortable, cozy goods, such as sweatpants. (This is another reason it was important I had great relationships with our vendors—I was able to get enough inventory of the cozy clothing our customers were demanding.)

Conventional thinking didn't consider asymmetric risk. I knew that if the government allowed us to reopen, there would be a tidal wave of pent-up demand. Over 400,000 people had fled Manhattan for the suburbs like the Hamptons, and they were itching to get out of their houses and pretend life was normal.

I took the risk and leased a smaller store, roughly eight hundred square feet of selling space, and filled it with only comfortable clothes from one of our key brands called Jac Parker, a luxury basics line. We called it "Jac Parker by Mixology Clothing Company." As part of the deal with the landlord, I also rented the two-bedroom apartment situated directly above the store, which the staff was able to use as they needed. I considered it a once-in-a-lifetime deal. It's incredibly difficult to get access to apartments and stores in affluent areas such as the Hamptons.

Again, the asymmetry existed, and I decided that renting this store and apartment was not going to be the reason Mixology went out of business. I crafted a favorable, short-term deal with the landlord that provided me the option to stay longer if it worked—and using that optionality, we opened the second Hampton store.

Once quarantine ended and people were allowed out of their houses, it was like a tidal wave hit our business. After three months of being locked in, everyone wanted to go out. Leaving the house and doing something "normal" such as shopping had become a luxury. At this point, most nonessential travel was still shut down, so the only option was to do things locally. Shopping became a novelty. When people walked into stores and had conversations with our staff or other customers, they felt normal for the first time in months. For the rest of 2020, many of our customers showered my front-line team with gratitude and thanks for opening up and allowing them to feel some sense of normalcy.

Because I took the risk of hiring, opening new locations, and not canceling orders, we had the inventory available to handle the wave of customers who were desperate for a sense of normalcy.

The risks paid off big time, unlike any other risk in my career. Mixology had a phenomenal summer of sales. As we crept into July, sales were still at an all-time high, and I knew it was time to go on the offense. I began to build out the next store in Oceanside, New York, and on Labor Day weekend, our new Oceanside store opened for business.[42]

As we came out of the worst of COVID, my team had grown with even stronger hires; we were getting inventory, and we had three more stores than we started with. During COVID, I went on a "crazy" hiring binge, hiring over ten high-level team members I never would have been able to recruit had their companies not been downsized. It was the polar opposite of our situation during Hurricane Sandy. We went into Sandy with six stores and came out of it with three. In that situation, we had to pull back or we would have gone out of business.

With COVID, I learned how to play the asymmetries, how to play the leverage, and how to make decisions around staffing, location, inventory, and processes in order to take advantage of the

---

[42] Oceanside was actually where we opened the very first Mixology store, but it was sadly lost in Hurricane Sandy. This opening was a homecoming for us.

opportunities being presented. (John Danaher calls this "new wave jiu jitsu." It's his philosophy that the best time to attack is when scrambling from a perceived weak position.)

The key lesson from these experiences isn't that I always make the right decisions; in fact, far from it. Throughout my career, I've encountered various missteps. I've hired individuals who weren't the right fit, taken on leases that didn't pan out, and even had to shut down stores. These aren't just mistakes; they're integral parts of my journey. The real takeaway here aligns with one of Mixology's core values, which I adapted from Josh Waitzkin's *The Art of Learning*: the concept of investing in loss.[43] It's about embracing and learning from the inevitable errors and misjudgments. The crucial aspect is to ensure these mistakes are not debilitating, allowing your business to survive and thrive. Opportunities for significant breakthroughs might arise only a few times in an entire career. The goal is to be prepared, through the wisdom gained from past mistakes, to grasp these opportunities firmly when they do appear.

Omnichannel Asymmetric Decisions

In 2008, my father made a pioneering investment in the first Mixology Clothing Company store. Remarkably, this initial investment was recouped within just three months by our former partners. Subsequently, we've

---

[43] Josh Waitzkin, *The Art of Learning: An Inner Journey to Optimal Performance*. New York: Free Press, 2007.

consistently observed that under proficient management and with adequate infrastructure, the capital invested in launching a new Mixology store is typically recovered within its first 12–18 months of operations. I had always been aware of this profitable return and attributed it confidently to our omnichannel business strategy—our integration of online and in-store sales.

Often, in the midst of business decision-making, you discover a remarkably effective strategy yet notice it's not widely discussed or recognized. It's when you stumble upon a piece in a trade journal, book, article, or class that you receive validation of the significance of your discovery.

This exact scenario unfolded at Mixology. When Allbirds went public in November 2021, they filed Form 10 with the SEC. Beyond financial details, this document offers profound insights into the operations of public companies. Those willing to delve into and parse this extensive documentation can uncover fascinating aspects of their business strategies.

Arya Sajedi, my business partner in ARC, possesses that patience. He shared their Form 10 filing with me, remarking, "Take a look at this. It's unbelievable. Allbirds is going public. Examine their strategy." Reading through the sections Arya highlighted, I felt a sense of validation—Allbirds' business plan mirrored ours:

> Our digital commerce experience is complemented by a thriving retail store

fleet. **With strong pre-COVID-19 unit economics, our store operations have historically been highly profitable, capital-efficient, and provided strong investment returns.** All U.S. stores that were operating in 2019 generated approximately $4.3 million in average unit volume, or AUV, in their first 12 months of operation, including the stores that had their first 12 months of sales affected by COVID-19 after March 2020. Based on this pre-COVID performance, we believe our new stores will be highly profitable, have attractive payback periods, serve as good capital investments, and be positioned well to take advantage of physical retail's recovery from the pandemic. While our store channel already generates strong results on a standalone basis, **the real power of our vertical retail strategy is the synergy between the physical and digital sides of our business.** This synergy takes the form of **increased brand awareness and website traffic in the regions where we open new stores, driving an overall lift in sales.** Furthermore, as we continue to grow our store footprint, we believe we will be able to expand our valuable multi-channel customer base. Across all cohorts and through June 30, 2021, **our multi-channel repeat customers, who represented 12% of our total repeat customers as of such date, on average spent approximately 1.5 times more than our single-channel repeat customers.**

As an example of the benefits of our vertical retail distribution strategy, our Boston Back Bay store **achieved standalone payback within eight months**. Furthermore, in the three months after our Boston Back Bay store opened in March 2019, the Boston DMA region saw a 15% increase in website traffic, an 83% increase in new customers and, ultimately, a 77% increase in overall net sales, as compared to a comparable control market.[44]

Allbirds' documents revealed their strategy as a direct-to-consumer, digitally native brand, venturing into physical retail. Crucially, their stores typically become profitable within the first year, also catalyzing new online market territories. Like us, Allbirds

---

[44] Allbirds, Inc. (August 31, 2021). *United States Securities and Exchange Commission Form S-1 Registration Statement.* Retrieved from Securities and Exchange Commission website: https://www.sec.gov/Archives/edgar/data/1653909/0001628280 21017824/allbirdss-1.htm

discovered that omnichannel shoppers—those engaging both online and in-store—are significantly more valuable, reflecting a deeper commitment to the brand.[45]

Realizing this, I understood that our approach was not only effective but also not unique to us. It's a viable model employed by successful enterprises. As I discussed in Chapter 9, it's crucial not to just monitor direct competitors but to observe the strategies of the industry's best. Often, this valuable information is tucked away in seemingly mundane investor reports.

The prospect of recouping an investment within the first year is extraordinary, especially when contrasted with my typical commercial real estate investments, which may take seven to ten years for full return on investment. Consider the asymmetry here: if opening a store costs $250,000, that's the maximum potential loss. However, if I recover this investment within the first year and successfully manage the business over the next decade, it becomes a lucrative, cash-generating asset for all those proceeding years.

This pattern of success has been consistent, fueling our decision to continue expanding. Although opening a second store in the Hamptons appeared reckless to my team, my father and I saw it as an unparalleled chance for exceptional deals. Confronted with this challenge, I weighed whether

---

[45] As of 2024, Allbirds' stock was trading in the pennies, proving that even once seemingly invincible companies valued at billions of dollars are not immune to negative economic realities.

investing $250,000 to open a store was worthwhile, knowing a correct execution could recoup the cost within a year. This is a gamble I was, and still am, prepared to take every time.

The opportunity was ours to seize. Amid widespread business closures, our willingness to risk personal capital to open new stores—when others were retrenching—could transform these ventures into our most lucrative investments. The worst-case scenario? A loss of $250,000, shuttered stores, and the embarrassment before friends and family. It's this fear of failure and ridicule that often deters people from taking risks.

Ultimately, others' opinions matter little. True commitment means fully embracing the venture. My wife often challenges me with, "What if it doesn't fail? What if you succeed?" It's a perspective too many overlook: the possibility that the risk could indeed lead to success.

Balance, however, is key. There are those who perennially bet on success, engaging in reckless gambles, often to their downfall. That's not the approach I advocate. Strategic, well-considered business decisions are not mere gambles—they are tactical maneuvers.

Mat Chat

Upon deciding to open those stores, our initial investment was immediately depleted, and the anticipated risk materialized. There are a hundred different ways I could have failed in the execution of these projects. The build could have cost triple what I estimated. The manager could have been the wrong hire. I could have bought too much inventory or the wrong type of inventory.

Anything could have gone wrong, but the moment I made the decision to take the risk was the moment I passed the point of no return. No one has a crystal ball. Every time you make a business decision, there's the possibility you will lose. And you will lose. No one has a perfect decision-making record.

Both SpaceX and Tesla almost went out of business several times. Elon Musk has said that he thought both companies had less than a 10 percent chance of success. Tesla was launched in 2008 during a global recession when GM and Chrysler were going bankrupt. Yet he invested 100 percent of his net worth into them—and even borrowed money from his family and friends—in order to make those businesses work.

Virtually every business has been on the verge of having to make tough decisions like these. If you've been doing the work, building muscle memory, and constantly expanding your knowledge, the right decision instantly comes to you.

The people around you might look at your entrepreneurial decision-making as crazy. They may never be able to understand it. That's because they're not in your shoes. They don't have the same kind of ownership mentality you do because it's not their business.

As I mentioned at the beginning of the chapter, everyone has a different relationship to risk. Some people find risk exciting, while others find risk gives them immense fear and anxiety. Even to this day, I'm not a natural risk taker, but my long study of jiu jitsu has given me a completely different appreciation for, and understanding of, risk. I now see asymmetries in everything I do—in fact, I find it exciting to look for and understand them.

Once you start to understand the principle of asymmetric risk, you begin to realize that you may not actually be taking as much risk as you thought. You'll find you have to push yourself to take more risks.

There's the other type of person, however, who takes too much risk. They're reckless with risk, constantly swinging for the fences and aiming to hit only home runs. In jiu jitsu, these white belts are usually the ones who are very athletic and strong, and they dive in headfirst like a charging bull. The problem is, if you're attacking with your head forward like a bull, you're going to get choked. These are also often the people who have many failed businesses.

There's one prevalent trait that distinguishes the people who learn and master jiu jitsu from the ones who give up. The ones who give up are the ones who don't understand the concept of investment in loss. They never learn from their mistakes. They have no problem taking risks—taking risks is easy—but mastering the sport (or business or activity) and understanding how to find success eludes them. You'll find these people bounce from sport to sport to sport: jiu jitsu to fencing to extreme skateboarding to hunting to baseball.

Using a baseball metaphor, I've seen this in business with the people who never want to hit a single. They don't want to learn the fundamentals and instead constantly swing for the fences. The problem is if they do hit a grand slam, it becomes harder and harder for them to be willing to accept that they eventually need to learn the fundamentals. Instead, they constantly chase the dopamine hit they got from the grand slam.

If they're unlucky enough to hit that grand slam early in their career, they find that hunting for their next grand slam becomes all-consuming, yet always further away, until they can't even hit a single.

I have seen several friends who made decisions early in their lives or careers, never thinking they'd be paying for it a decade down the road. A deal is signed with someone who's a little bit shady because of a split-second decision, and nothing more is heard about it for years. Then, five or ten years later, that decision comes back to haunt them. (I've noticed this seems to happen most often to the people who have a "fake it 'till you make it" mentality.) The biggest risk-takers become risk averse, which is a travesty.

There are people on the other side of the risk spectrum too. I've found that I'm too comfortable with hitting singles. When I was nineteen years old, a mentor asked me, "What's the difference between a million-dollar real estate deal and a hundred-million-dollar real estate deal?"

Me: I don't know.

Mentor: There is no difference. It's just zeroes. The paperwork is the same. Insurance is the same. The lease is the same. Everything about doing the deal is the same except one thing: your desire and ability to take the risk associated with losing your or your investor's money.

Unlike then, I've now signed hundreds of leases, raised tens of millions of dollars, opened dozens of stores, and hired and fired thousands of employees. Today when I take a risk, the asymmetry that exists for my investors is my experience.

Whether you're risk averse or too risky, asymmetries exist that you can use to make risk work for you, as long as you remember that asymmetric risk is not reckless risk.

Chapter 11
Control

A note before we begin: when we discuss control in this chapter, it's important to know I'm referring to items in your control. By having tight control over the things in your life that can be controlled, you gain mastery over the uncontrollable. I'm not advocating for controlling people or power. Follow the serenity prayer: "God, grant me the serenity to accept the things I cannot change, the courage to change the things I can, and the wisdom to know the difference."

When asked what Brazilian jiu jitsu is, John Danaher said:

> Brazilian Jiu-Jitsu (BJJ) is a grappling-based martial art whose central theme is the skill of controlling a resisting opponent in ways that force him to submit. Due to the fact that control is generally easier on the ground than in a standing position, much of the technique of Brazilian Jiu-Jitsu (BJJ) is centered around the skill of taking an

opponent down to the ground and wrestling for dominant control positions from where the opponent can be rendered harmless. To control and overcome greater size, strength, and aggression with lesser size and strength is the keynote of the sport. This is done by utilizing superior leverage, grip, and position upon your opponent.[46]

In a nutshell, jiu jitsu is about exerting your control over another person. When asked why effective control is so important, John Danaher uses the metaphor of a cowboy wrangling a steer. The cowboy uses a rope to bring the steer to the ground, and as soon as that steer is down, they tie its legs in order to exert control over the steer's movements and avoid getting kicked in the face.

The same principle is used in jiu jitsu. When exerting control over an opponent, the goal is to take them to the ground, get around their dangerous legs, and then use a system of pins and controls in order to assert dominance.

In the last chapter, we discussed the importance of asymmetric risk, which is taking risks that are proportionate to the outcomes you desire. Sometimes those risks are calculated, and sometimes the odds are stacked against you. No matter how calculated or

---

[46] "What Is Brazilian Jiu-Jitsu (BJJ)?," Renzo Gracie Academy, https://renzogracieacademy.com/about/what-is-brazilian-jiu-jitsu-bjj/.

stacked, you need to find a way to win.

Jiu Jitsu Principle: Control for Submission

It's often said that in the UFC (and the sport of mixed martial arts), style makes fights. Yet someone who looks untouchable as a striker, who's been knocking out opponent after opponent, can fight a wrestler who drops them to the ground immediately and controls the rest of the fight. In modern mixed martial arts history, the person who most embodies this is Khabib Nurmagomedov, who was known as the most dominant, most controlling, and least struck fighter of all time.

To the outsider, Khabib's fights could seem boring because he didn't utilize the big striking kicks and flashy techniques that spectators love to watch. Instead, he utilized absolute control, dragging his opponents into deep, deep metaphorical waters. Having another person physically control you feels suffocating, and his opponents often gave up because of it.

I often talk about control through the lens of risk. Remember, you're never more vulnerable than when you take a risk. Imagine going for a submission, like a triangle choke, and when you throw up your legs, it doesn't quite work out. Your opponent throws your legs out of the way and passes to side control or mount. It's a setback, and it can be disheartening.

On the flip side, when a risk pays off, it's not time to

kick back. Successfully navigating a risk can often lead to complacency, underestimating the ongoing challenges that lie ahead.

In the rematch between Matt Hughes and Frank Trigg at UFC 52 on April 16, 2005, the dynamics of control within a fight were on stark display. Early in the bout, Hughes was compromised by an accidental knee to the groin that went unnoticed by the referee, allowing Trigg to capitalize on Hughes's momentary weakness. Trigg aggressively pursued the advantage, taking Hughes to the ground and applying a rear-naked choke that seemed to signal a near-certain victory.

However, the fight took a dramatic turn when Hughes managed to escape the choke, demonstrating not only his resilience but also the unpredictable nature of control in mixed martial arts. In a display of strength and strategy, Hughes lifted Trigg off the ground, carried him across the Octagon, and executed a powerful slam. This move shifted the momentum entirely, allowing Hughes to take a dominant position. He then applied his own rear-naked choke, forcing Trigg to submit.

This bout between Hughes and Trigg is a clear illustration of how control in a fight can change hands in an instant. Despite being on the verge of defeat, Hughes's ability to reverse his fortunes and secure a win underlines the importance of resilience, technique, and seizing opportunities when they arise.

Control is essential—but elusive. It's fickle. It can be taken from you in a second. You think you have it in your grasp, and you're on top of the world because your risks paid off, but in your haste, you go for the win too fast. This gives up control and lets your opponent gain ground back. The art of jiu jitsu is how to keep control, which ultimately leads to submission, your desired outcome.

Trigg was winning the fight and moments away from victory but didn't finish the submission—and then froze because he didn't apply the technique properly. He went from having control to losing control. Hughes, on the other hand, was able to escape, explode with technique developed from decades of experience, establish control, apply his own rear-naked choke, and finish Trigg, leading to the win.

One of the aspects that will lead you to win is strong posture and tight body connection. To excel, you must learn how to use all your limbs in concert. The goal is to use every single resource—all your fingers, all your toes, your legs, your heels, even your chin—to exert control over your opponent.

I once had the opportunity to train with Eddie Cummings, a student of John Danaher and a pioneer of the Danaher Death Squad. When Eddie and the rest of the Death Squad came on the competition scene, they quickly dismantled everyone they came up against, even renowned professional jiu jitsu fighters who had been training for decades.

During our round, I found that Eddie used his head as a fifth limb in a way I had never felt, been taught, or even heard about. He was significantly smaller than me, in both height and weight, and yet it felt as if I was completely immobilized by his ability to control me.

When he stood over me and attacked my open guard, he used his head to pin me where my carotid artery is located in the neck. I was shocked at how heavy he felt for a person so much smaller than me, a feat he was able to accomplish because of the control he was exerting over me. In order to get that control, Eddie had to have a tight body connection and strong posture.

A strong posture fortifies one's defenses effectively. It's akin to being well rooted, much like a tree. Trees with deep and firm roots withstand countless hurricanes, undeterred by the fiercest winds. Similarly, a strong posture empowers you to attack with greater confidence and control. Conversely, a weak foundation, akin to poor posture, leaves you vulnerable and easily destabilized due to a lack of grounding.

On the other hand, excessive rigidity or stiffness can be a downfall. Just as a tree's survival in a hurricane is owed to both its deep roots and its flexibility, rigidity can lead to being uprooted. Hence, the ideal is a balance: a posture that is both strong and adaptable.

Consider John Danaher's illustration involving a cowboy and a steer. If the steer charges headlong, head down, the cowboy can simply sidestep and lasso it. But if the steer remains alert, keeping its head up and maintaining an upright posture, roping it becomes significantly more challenging.

Maintaining a raised head and a firm posture can preemptively counteract threats. The steer becomes vulnerable only when it charges with lowered head and horns. In a clash with another bull, this might be less risky, but against a skilled cowboy, the danger escalates. Posture, in essence, is about restraint, caution, and bodily control, mitigating the inherent risks of aggression.

Effective posture is also crucial in weight distribution. Fighters, through bodily mastery, can make themselves feel extraordinarily heavy to their opponents. Casual UFC viewers often wonder why a fighter doesn't simply shove their opponent away and stand up; the answer lies in the opponent's control over both the fighter's body and, consequently, their weight.

As I've pointed out previously, those unfamiliar with jiu jitsu often oversimplify ground fights. They claim, "I would just stand up," "I would push them off," or "I would bite and escape." However, experienced jiu jitsu fighters understand the complexity and challenge of these situations.

This analogy extends to the business world. When businesses are burdened by external factors like government regulations, competition, or pandemics, simplistic advice like "Why don't you just stay in business?" can be frustratingly naïve. The reality is often more complex, especially for those still learning. Businesses can be constrained by various circumstances—legalities, quarantines, supply chain issues—without yet having devised strategies to navigate these challenges.

Business Principle: Exerting Control and Controlling Advantage

At this point in the pandemic, we had successfully navigated through the challenges and obstacles using every bit of wit and wisdom we had learned in the years spent creating business muscle memory. As our customers came out of their houses, we made calculated risks that immediately began to work.

Only a few short months before, we could have potentially gone out of business like the seven hundred thousand other businesses in the US (a number that's surpassed three million as of 2024), but instead, our decisions were paying off. It was now a time to be hypervigilant, watch every dollar spent, and pay extreme attention to detail so we didn't ruin the opportunity we had fought so hard to gain.

The year before legendary 49ers coach Bill Walsh took over the team, their record was 2–14. In his first year as coach (1979), they again lost fourteen games. Two seasons later, in 1981, they won the Super Bowl. How does a team go from losing well over half their games to winning the Super Bowl in only two years? By focusing on the minutiae. He implemented Standards of Performance. According to Ryan Holiday in *Ego Is the Enemy*, "The Standard of Performance was about instilling excellence. These seemingly simple but exacting standards matter more than some grand vision or power trip. In his eyes, if the players take care of the details, 'the score takes care of itself.' The winning would happen."[47]

On any given day, any professional team could beat any other professional team. What separates the absolute best is how they approach and focus on the tiny details.

You can see this in jiu jitsu when you study Khabib. He's not throwing around fancy techniques or doing triple roundhouse kicks like you see in Jackie Chan movies. He focuses on control. He uses fundamental grappling techniques to exert extreme leverage and pinning pressure over his opponents. This focus on control is what's needed to be successful in business as well.

When you come out on the other side of a risk and find you've been successful, it can be surprising. It happens to me all the time. I've been in business long enough to find things go wrong more often than they go right. In jiu jitsu, I've tapped thousands of times more than I've submitted. Even as a higher belt, you'll find you fail more than you succeed (and if that is not the case, you are in the wrong arena).

It's rare to get a one-punch knockout, so when you do, it's critical to stop your ego from taking over. Instead, I suggest you fall back on your fundamentals—the muscle memory that made you successful in the first place. As my dad likes to say, "Don't read your own headlines."

It can be hard once people get a little bit of fame

---

[47] Ryan Holiday, *Ego Is the Enemy*. New York: Penguin Random House, 2016.

and notoriety. You get mentioned in the newspaper or win business of the year. That's fantastic, absolutely. But how did you get there in the first place? What were you doing all those years leading up to that moment of success? How much work were you putting in? How early were you getting up? Don't forget to keep utilizing those techniques and habits while basking in the glow of the limelight.

Post-lockdown, Mixology was realizing incredible success. We were shocked at how many customers came back right away, but we were prepared for it. As we talked about in the previous chapters, we nurtured and kept our best people on board, and we made sure that our top employees didn't kill and eat our bottom employees (and trust me, they tried) because we were thinking six months ahead. Believing the government was going to let us reopen, it was imperative that we made sure we had enough people to run our stores when they opened. (It's easy to forget that while you want Michael Jordan, you also need the towel boy.)

Because we took those risks, we were able to exert the proper control over the business.

A common adage in business is "having your finger on the pulse." When you have your finger on the pulse of a person, you're checking to see if they're alive. When you have a finger on the pulse of your business, the understanding is that you know what's making things happen in your business.

When you're an entrepreneur, you're expected to know a lot about a lot of things and leverage your team to fill in your gaps. With so much to keep track of, it can be very easy to lose control. Business can be ruthless. No one is going to have a pity party for you when things aren't going your way.

Having control over your business requires incredible mastery over many things, including relying on, trusting, and empowering other people to help you. I've often found that when people reach the end of their natural capacity—meaning how much they can do with their time—it's difficult for them to give up control in order to reach the next level.

For example, imagine you're speeding down the highway and drive over a pothole. Would you screech to a halt, get out of your car, and start stomping your feet and screaming, "Why is there a pothole here? Why hasn't anyone filled it in?" Of course not. You would simply continue speeding along. The best entrepreneurs don't let potholes stop them from moving their business forward. **When solo entrepreneurs and small business owners come to me for advice on a problem, generally, they're metaphorically screaming at a pothole instead of charging forward.**

Part of establishing control means both understanding what you're going through and looking into the future, weighing how one decision will affect the next decision. If you're in a fight, control is not just about stopping their motion. It's also about redirecting all their motion.

People often think control is about using brute strength to hold their opponent down. Control is leading all their actions so that they are completely immobilized. Every inch they try to take you have an answer for.

In business, it's about redirecting no matter what twists and turns come your way. If a police officer tells you to shut it down, you say, "No problem, officer." If an employee comes into your office, you expect them to be upset.

If you do not control your business, your expenses are going to run away from you. You'll spend too much on things you shouldn't have bought. Your employees will go rogue if they don't have great leadership. Control allows you to take risks that become wins you expected.

What You Can't Afford

In December of 2021, I promoted Eugene to CFO of Mixology Clothing Company—a well-earned title. Remember, Eugene was originally hired in 2016 as our controller, after twelve failed bookkeeper hires over a three-year period. Eugene was out of my ideal budget, but I took the risk to hire him anyway.

My philosophy was this: if I have a million-dollar problem, I have to assign the right resources to solve it. Once it's solved, I will have more than enough budget to pay for the problem. The budget doesn't exist until the problem is fixed. If I'm not performing the way I want, I have to attack the problem in a way that I'm not attacking the problem now. Sometimes, that means taking a risk and exerting myself beyond where I'm comfortable in order to solve the issue.

When I met Eugene, I was candid with my expectations: "I can't teach you anything about bookkeeping, accounting, or how to be a controller. You have to come to this job with the knowledge of how to execute at a high level. I can help you understand the fashion retail business, but you're going to have to bring the accounting knowledge and **reconcile the cash every day**." (Businesses generally fail when they run out of working capital—i.e., run out of cash—so being able to manage cash inflow and outflow is critical to staying in control of your business.)

Eugene didn't blink as he replied, "I'm the man for the job."

In his first year, Eugene saved Mixology a million dollars by doing one thing: controlling our expenses. Think of your business as a beautiful ship. It may have gorgeous, handcrafted molding, a high-end navigation system, and an incredible crew, but without an engineer (i.e., controller) to plug the leaks and stop new ones from starting, your ship is eventually going to sink. If you have leaks, you don't need to buy a whole new boat. You simply need to find the right person to plug them.

There are certain expenses in your business that are variable, so they can be managed by a controller like Eugene, while other expenses are fixed. Your job as owner is to make sure that you get the best price possible for the fixed expenses before they become fixed and rely on your controller (or accounting professional) to control the variable expenses.

(Please know, my examples below are strictly for

Mixology. Every business is different, and every industry is different; therefore, everyone will have different fixed and variable expenses. I highlight the following anecdote to illustrate a philosophy more than a business how-to. Other industries and business categories, like service businesses, will have different financial levers. The core insight I wish to impart—having excellent financial controls and live financial data will help you win—is industry agnostic.)

The first and most important expense to control in the fashion retail business is your purchasing, meaning how much inventory you buy and how much of your inventory you're selling. The second biggest expense generally is your people. If you can control your payroll as a percentage of sales, you can start to control the business.

The next expense to control is your rent. My job as CEO is to write good deals for our leases, as once they're written, they become (relatively) fixed expenses, and there's not much you can control. Instead, the control happens at lease negotiation: knowing the current state of your business and how much potential business you can do in that lease's market.

There are other expenses to control—marketing, professional services, fees, travel, food, supplies, etc.—but they are minuscule compared to purchasing, payroll, and rent. With Eugene's expertise, we are able to control what goes on in every location and can see "in the numbers" which areas of the business are successful and which are not.

I've spoken with too many entrepreneurs who are singularly focused on getting their small businesses to the next level. They've reached the $1 or $2 million mark, and they want to grow more, but they're doing everything themselves. I've tried to explain that they need to hire a controller or a better accountant, but too often the response is: "I can't afford to hire a controller," or "I can't afford an accountant." They don't understand that they can't afford *not* to hire these people. If the foundation of a business is never built, there's no control, and like a house of cards, it will eventually fall down.

Businesses with loose financial practices are unlikely to survive. Similar to jiu jitsu, you need to have strong fundamental controls. In business, you use math and fundamental business techniques. The earliest known examples of human writing are receipts, dating back approximately twelve thousand years, inscribed on rocks and stone fragments.

Control over your business is as old as the written word.

Mat Chat

The reason jiu jitsu has been so powerful for me in business is because it has taught me how to exercise control over all of the circumstances of my life. As Viktor Frankl says, "You cannot control what happens to you in life, but you can always control what you will feel and do about what happens to you."[48] Now, I may not be able to control the ocean, but I can control how I surf through it. If I fall off the board, I can get back on it. Sometimes I may have to tap out and try again tomorrow.

Jiu jitsu teaches you how to accept that you are being controlled *and* how to control the circumstances that are happening around you.

Control over your circumstances can also be found through learning. The journey of an entrepreneur can be isolating and lonely. It can feel like you're always on the bottom, always getting submitted, always getting beat up. Turning to books, I found both camaraderie and a measure of control over my circumstances by learning about all the other founders, generals, athletes, coaches, and businesspeople, old and young, dead and alive, who had been through the same situations I was going through. After all, if they were able to make it through, why couldn't I?

It's risky to start a business. As we have discussed, the US Bureau of Labor Statistics reports that 20 percent of new businesses fail during the first two years of being open, 45 percent during the first five years, and 65 percent during the first ten years. In the dark of night, when you don't know if your risk is going to pay off, if you've made the right decisions, you can either get lost in spiraling thoughts, or you could get lost in the pages of a book (or podcast or audiobook).

---

[48] Viktor E. Frankl, *Man's Search for Meaning*. Boston: Beacon Press, 2006.

When I advise you to have control over all your muscles, remember that your brain is a muscle too. Control over your thoughts and emotions is just as important as control over your body. If you don't have control over your emotions, you're most likely going to make poor decisions, and one bad decision leads to the next and the next and the next.

If you feel that you don't have control over your business, I would also advise you to become obsessed with the fundamentals of every part of business. You don't have to be an accountant or know how to file a tax return, but you need to know how accounting affects your business so that you can have conversations with your accountants, controllers, and landlords. You don't have to be a real estate attorney, but you should know how leases work.

Just because you took an accounting class in college doesn't mean you should never take an accounting class again. I've taken three accounting classes since college, and each time, I learned something new because my perspective and experience have changed. Each time you retake a class, you filter the information through those new perspectives and experiences, which gives you new insight and deeper understanding.

(As a reminder, I call this a technical framework: learn a technique, drill the technique, use the technique in live sparring, discuss the technique and its core insights in a mat chat, and then repeat, year after year. It is one of the core tenets of my jiu jitsu practice that I brought with me to business.)

Everything you learn becomes fuel to help you grow your business. And every single time you practice one of these teachings, you understand more about how to exert control over the circumstances of your life.

I don't know a single successful entrepreneur or businessperson who doesn't love to read. Why? Because that's where the answers are. Great entrepreneurs love to increase their knowledge because they know they need to be dangerous at every single part of business, just as mixed martial arts champions need to know multiple styles such as jiu jitsu, judo, kickboxing, wrestling, and so on.

However, remember that control is not about mastery but about practice. It's too easy to forget, as you gain experience, that you were once a white belt. If you're doing it right, you should constantly be putting yourself in a position where you're still tapping, still learning, and still finding room to grow. Just as those great entrepreneurs and professionals I spoke about above are not just voracious readers, they also put what they learn into practice every day.

In both fighting and business, it's essential to have a fundamental understanding of each facet within your domain. As you persevere year after year, soaking up more knowledge, you methodically level up. Once you have mastered the art of control, you can go for the submission victory.

Chapter 12
Finishing Principles

In Chapter 5, we talked about three types of fear that hold people back: the fear of starting, the fear of continuing, and the fear of finishing. If you're at the point where you are considering finishing tactics, you are a very special person. Fine-tuning the way that you learn to finish, whether that's closing deals or winning matches, puts you in a very special category: people who finish.

We've talked several times about the washout rate in jiu jitsu and entrepreneurship. The people who get to the point where they're able to fine-tune their finishing tactics are incredibly rare. Many people fall prey to the fear of finishing and never finish at all.

In 2016, a video of a young man attempting to break a board, a common practice in karate, went viral.[49] In a room full of parents and fellow students, he stepped up to the board being held by Jason Wilson, the

---

[49] The Cave of Adullam (@Cave313), "Breaking Through Emotional Barriers," filmed July 26, 2016. YouTube Video, 5:25, https://youtu.be/ooAOc9Fwg0U?si=mP6qliUQ4_fqg2b5.

founder of the Cave of Adullam Transformational Training Academy, an organization that uses martial arts to empower young Black men. As the child began to strike, he pulled his punch and punched at the board instead of through the board.

Similar to following through in your golf, baseball, or tennis swing, in martial arts, you're trained to punch all the way through the target. The same principle applies to business: when an opportunity presents itself, are you pulling your punch, or are you following through?

Jiu Jitsu Principle: Deciding to Finish

When John Danaher teaches jiu jitsu, he emphasizes training students to secure victories through submission finishes, irrespective of the rule set. John believes that the true spirit of sport jiu jitsu lies in actively seeking and achieving submissions. He believes matches should be approached with this submission-focused mindset.

One of the most prominent jiu jitsu organizations, the International Brazilian Jiu Jitsu Federation (IBJJF), uses a point system that inadvertently encourages many competitors to game the rules in order to win rather than playing to the nature of the martial art. Because of this, some athletes develop a style of stalling and gathering points instead of taking a risk and going for submission victories.

When we're in a training environment and facing the same people we train with every night, getting to know each other's styles and tactics inside and out, it can become difficult to be a finisher—especially because finishing is difficult to do in general. Developing finishing tactics and techniques is very technical and, surprising to many practitioners, includes a mental component (the fear of finishing that we discussed in Chapter 5).

Some people are naturally predisposed to finishing; they're born with this "killer instinct." These are Michael-Jordan-wanting-the-ball-type people. Yet I've found that the majority of people are not born with this instinct. I definitely wasn't. However, I was able to hone a killer instinct over time. You can see this with big cats. When they're young, tigers pounce on and bite at their parents. While it looks like they're simply playing, their parents are actually teaching them to hone their killer instincts.

We talked in Chapter 5 about how many people have a hard time starting, and there have been many books and articles written about how to start a project or business or idea. Yet the topic of finishing principles is spoken about much less often, both because it's an abstract concept and because it's unbelievably difficult to master.

In the book *Sword and Brush* by Dave Lowry, he talks about the principle of *yoyu,* or critical margin.[50] He describes yoyu as the moment where a samurai decides whether or not they will take someone's life with their sword. He also tells the legend of a samurai

---

[50] Dave Lowry, Sword and Brush: *The Spirit of the Martial Arts* (Boulder, CO: Shambhala, 1995).

who, while demonstrating their abilities, would put a grain of rice on a willing participant's forehead and, with a full stroke of the sword, cut the rice without damaging the person.

The principle of yoyu can sometimes be mistranslated or misunderstood to mean pulling your punch, as the boy did in the Cave of Adullam video. However, there's a tremendous difference between pulling your punch and not finishing. Pulling your punch is subconsciously stopping yourself from hitting through the board and finishing, while yoyu is having complete mastery over your ability to decide if and when you are going to finish.

When I began my jiu jitsu journey, I watched fighters utilize these finishing techniques in the UFC and tried to replicate those body movements in order to mimic what I thought was happening. Given my inexperience with the techniques at that stage, it's unsurprising that my early attempts failed. This was a classic case of the Dunning-Kruger effect in action: my lack of knowledge led to me overestimating my ability to replicate the techniques. It wasn't until I dedicated more time to learning the fundamental principles that I realized the difficulty of what I had been trying to imitate.

As I traveled further down the path of jiu jitsu practice and started to get more and more submission finishes, I found something else could happen. When you begin to compete against people at the same level or higher than you, you'll find yourself in situations where you can go in for the submission—but sometimes, there's something holding you back from being able to take the win.

Business Principle: Closing Deals, Tracking Change, and Leveraging People

The fear of finishing is something I see almost daily in business. Too many times, I've had someone come into my office and ask for a raise or promotion, and as soon as I'm ready to give it to them, they realize that now they have to do the work that comes with the opportunity.

Take a real estate agent, for example. They do the legwork to find a client and get the listing, but then they have to sell that house. There's a big difference between going out to get the lead and going out to close the deal.

Closing a deal is nuanced. You may have used the information in Chapter 9 to create a dilemma, which sets you up for the win, but then you still have to close the deal. However, there are so many different personalities involved in a transaction—lawyers, buyers, sellers, insurance brokers—and any one of those people can ruin the deal.

You would think that everyone involved would want to get the deal done—would be incentivized to get the deal done—but the reality is that everyone involved wants to make the most money that they possibly can. That's what often ends up killing deals. Everyone has opinions, and everyone wants more, so getting everyone on the same page is a huge challenge. The reason dealmakers make big money is because it is so hard to get deals closed.

It can still be difficult to close because the art of finishing is incredibly difficult. In my experience, the biggest obstacle to closing a deal is usually the person themselves. It's like the young boy punching the board, trying to break it. It's not the person holding the board's fault; it's not the people in the room's fault, and it's not his teammates' fault—it's the boy not having the courage, the confidence, to punch through the board.

The art of punching through the board was not the difficult part for him. He had done it before over and over again in practice. But when he stepped up in front of a large crowd, with his parents and coach watching, the pressure was overwhelming, and he pulled his punch.

Being able to close the deal is one of the things that separates the highest-performing people in the world from those who can do a lot of work exceptionally well, except for the most important work.

For Mixology Clothing Company, Eugene and I break the business down for each of the store managers into seven key indicators on a daily, weekly, monthly, and yearly basis. These key indicators are sales, payroll, cleanliness, social media/marketing, customer information capture, clienting, and merchandising. Each of these indicators, if done well, indicates success.

Some of my managers have the killer instinct that makes them so good at closing the deal when selling that the other six areas naturally fall in line. For the managers who don't have that natural sales instinct, they need to focus more on the other key indicators. Unfortunately, sometimes the managers who struggle with sales either become so hyper-focused on the other six areas that they forget to focus on the most important area—selling—or they force sales to prove that they aren't struggling.

In the fashion retail business, you're there to service the customer's needs. Usually, when a customer comes into a store, they need something, and it comes down to your ability as a salesperson to navigate them through the store to get them what they need. Managers who are trying to get to the next level can sometimes begin to oversell their customers.

Think of someone in jiu jitsu who is learning dangerous submission techniques and hurting their training partners. If you hurt your training partner, they're not going to train with you again. If you oversell a customer because you're only thinking about your goals that day, they're very unlikely to come back.

A good team member or manager aims to meet the customer's wants and needs, ensuring they return regularly—weekly, monthly, and annually. Repeat customers are invaluable; they have a deep understanding of your brand and loyalty toward you. They are also more inclined to recommend you to their network. The ultimate objective is to cultivate a base of repeat customers and create numerous opportunities for their return.

When I coach managers who aren't hitting their

sales goals, they often say, "I can make big sales. I made a $300 sale," "I made a $800 sale," or "I made a $2,000 sale." I nod, and then ask, "But did that customer come back? Did they walk out of the store feeling amazing, or did they feel like you took advantage of them?"

Managers who have a hard time understanding this nuance of finishing tend to find that their repeat customer metrics continually decrease, and they don't understand why they're not creating authentic relationships with the customers. They don't realize that making the sale is not the job; the job is to create trust so the customer comes back over and over.

In his book *The 7 Habits of Highly Effective People,* Stephen Covey says the second habit is to begin with the end in mind.[51] Too often people (usually beginners or intermediates) start something without knowing how they want to finish. Remember our pothole analogy? If you don't know your end goal, it's easy to get upset about the details. Anything that stands in the way of the goal is a small obstacle that should never be a reason to not finish. If you dig your heels in on every single part of the deal, the deal will fall apart.

Masters, on the other hand, have been down the road so many times that they know most, if not all, of the potential pathways and how to connect different ones to get to the right finish. They don't get hung up on the small obstacles because they remember the

---

[51] Stephen R. Covey, *The 7 Habits of Highly Effective People* (Provo, UT: Franklin Covey, 1998).

reason they are here is to finish.

When he was still competing, Rickson Gracie said he went from step one to step two to step three, and when he reached step three, he would never go back to step two. What he meant was that as he began to utilize techniques on his opponents, he was breaking down their defenses one at a time, leading them down a path to submission. By both knowing all the different tactics his opponents could do in response to his actions and knowing his end goal was to finish with submission, he was almost always able to adapt and overcome in order to win the match.

You can also see the difference in finishing with marathon runners. Some runners appear composed the entire race, but with only one hundred feet to go, their bodies collapse to the ground, and they crawl toward the finish line on their hands and knees. Other runners sail through the finish line with no problem. Rich Roll talks about why this happens in his book *Finding Ultra.*[52]

Rich wanted to become an ultra-marathon runner, so he hired a running coach who told him that even though he was fast and strong, he needed to slow down in his training. Even if you can run a six-minute mile, that doesn't mean you should when it comes to marathon training. Instead, you should run a much slower mile in training in order to run faster on race

---

[52] Rich Roll, *Finding Ultra: Rejecting Middle Age, Becoming One of the World's Fittest Men, and Discovering Myself* (New York, NY: Harmony Books, 2018).

day.

This might sound like common sense, but it can be difficult to follow during an actual race. When my wife ran the Paris Marathon, there were drummers and DJs and confetti and cheering people at almost every mile marker. The excitement and energy levels were sky high. But when you're training for the marathon, you're generally out there on the road alone. While the goal is to do in the marathon what you practiced at home, it's impossible to practice for all that excitement and energy.

When you are filled with excitement, energy, and nerves, it's easy to come out of the gate hot, and before you know it, instead of running an eight-and-a-half-minute mile, you just ran a six-and-a-half-minute mile. This is most often seen with beginners and runners who don't begin with the end in mind. Unfortunately, it's extremely hard to recover once you've expended all that energy, and you find yourself approaching the finish line with an empty tank.

These same issues can happen in the business world. The difference is that these lessons take shape over many months or even years, and if you don't know how to look out for them, you can find yourself burned out and unable to close the deal on an amazing opportunity even if you're right at the finish line.

Tracking for Change

When you show up to jiu jitsu practice on a nightly basis without actively seeking to maximize each training session, you can find yourself training for years without seeing much improvement. I made this mistake myself when I was a white belt and at the start of my blue belt. But when I started taking my training more seriously toward the end of my blue belt, I had a mission. I started studying tapes of different matches. I took notes on each night's session. I spent time thinking about my submissions and rolling sessions. I considered how I was getting into certain positions and utilizing certain techniques. I asked myself, "Why did this happen?" for both the good and bad.

I was beginning with the end in mind. I became, and still am, very intentional with what I was doing in jiu jitsu and in my life.

Every Friday, I do a review of my entire week in my journal and give myself a score. (You can access my planner scoring system using the link in the Resources section at the end of the book.) In my weekly planner, I list all the things I have to do down the left side of the page. On the right side are boxes for Monday, Tuesday, Wednesday, Thursday, and Friday. When I do the task, I put a dot in the box for that day. If I didn't do it, I put an X in the box for that day. If I get to the end of the week and see four Xs for a task, I am absolutely going to take care of that task on Friday.

At the end of the workday on Friday, I create my list for the following week. I also spend time thinking about any items I didn't finish. Is there a reason I didn't do them? Am I waiting on someone to be able to do an item? When I'm building my list, I also take stock of any other projects or events going on. I make sure to check in with all the key people who report to me to ensure they don't need anything from me and I don't need anything from them.

If I'm building a store or trying to close a deal, I have a whole list of questions I ask myself. Did I check in with the contractors? Did I speak to my attorney? Did I speak to my banker? Did I speak to the opposing side? Is there anyone else involved who I need to call or check in with? Is there any paperwork I need to finalize?

By wrapping up my week on Friday, I'm ensuring my entire next week is already prepped. When I walk into my office on Monday morning, I already know, beyond a shadow of a doubt, the highest-priority task that I need to accomplish first.

However, I don't only track my business tasks. I also record any habits or personal projects that are important to me. Am I eating healthy? Did I intermittent fast that day? How many hours did I fast? How much water did I drink? Did I read? When I was working toward my MBA, I tracked if I worked on that. Did I work on the *Business Jiu Jitsu* podcast? Did I work on this book? Did I train at the dojo that day? Did I do cardio, weightlifting, or cross-training at the gym? I even keep a list of the friends and family I intentionally want to keep in my life and track how often I make plans with them.

Every single aspect of my life is on this page. Every single week I print it out and update it to make sure that I am intentional about beginning with the end in mind for everything in my life. This is how I ensure nothing slips through the cracks. If I do something, I mark it off. If I don't do something, I don't mark it off so I have an honest assessment of my week every week.

This is the life and business system I developed so that I can manage hundreds of people across multiple different businesses and keep it all straight. It would be impossible to keep all of this in my head.

I developed this system over many years and without much input. However, just like the Allbirds Form 10 gave me validation about my business plan at Mixology, I picked up a copy of the *Checklist Manifesto* by Atul Gawande and learned about how surgeons and airline pilots use checklists just like mine to win. It was validation and fuel that helped me refine and improve my process.

> "Finding a good idea is apparently not all that hard. Finding an entrepreneur who can execute a good idea is a different matter entirely. One needs a person who can take an idea from proposal to reality, work the long hours, build a team, handle the pressures and setbacks, manage technical and people problems alike, and stick with the effort for years on end without getting distracted or going insane. Such people are rare and extremely hard to spot."
> — Atul Gawande, *The Checklist Manifesto: How to Get Things Right*

What I've learned through jiu jitsu is how important it is to have a technical framework and a systems-based approach to be able to finish. After all, that's what jiu jitsu is. It's a technical system consisting of learning, practicing, and using techniques in order to learn how to finish.

Keep in mind, however, that when I first started learning about principles like yoyu, many of them flew right over my head. I didn't have a frame of reference to understand a nuanced principle like this yet. After all, if you don't know how to finish people with technique, how can you truly understand? If you're really smart, you may be able to conceptually understand the idea of yoyu. But it's not until you've put in the time to learn and practice the principles and nuances of how to finish (remember that muscle memory) that you are able to finish more consistently.

The purpose of keeping track of everything in my life in the short term, near term, and long term is so I can finish everything. Many of us, especially entrepreneurs, daydream about all the ideas and things we want to do in our lives. "I want to see this person." "I want to do that." "I should have done this." "I should have done that." Tony Robbins calls this "should-ing all over yourself."

The question I get asked most often is, "How do you do it all? How do you run multiple businesses, keep up jiu jitsu, have a social life, write books, and earn your MBA? How can you do all these things and do them pretty well?" Hopefully, you've realized by this point in the book that I've tapped millions of times, and I've failed millions of times in order to get to this point of success.

That said, there is an answer to this question:

leverage.

Leverage

One of the ways you learn to become a good finisher is through the use of leverage. We first learn about leverage as little kids on a seesaw, using weight to raise and lower each other. In elementary school, we learn about pulleys, cranes, and forklifts and the idea that if we want to get big jobs done, we need to use tools. This basic principle helps us throughout life in many different ways.

In business, being able to leverage the talents of other people is critical. Even if you're a solo entrepreneur, you need to cooperate with others to perform tasks outside of your discipline, such as having your taxes done or a legal contract written. Every entrepreneur quickly finds that working with teams benefits them.

In jiu jitsu, you need to leverage your teammates during practice in order to improve. It would be virtually impossible (there's always an exception to every rule) to become an ADCC champion if you never trained with another person.

Leveraging the talent, hard work, and loyalty of the people around you in order to amplify what you want to do often brings success. In the US Army Special Forces, they call this force multiplication. US Army Rangers are typically trained to speak multiple languages, and with limited resources, a handful of them can go into a foreign land and work with a much less-equipped militia or army to create a guerrilla force. They do this to maximal effect by sharing knowledge and weapon skills with a group of willing participants who can then effect change in their area.

The challenge is when you have the best of the best forced to work with people they see as beneath them. Your A players always want to work with other A players. But even on the dream team, there's going to be someone who's the best and someone who's the worst. Your job as the leader is to get your entire team working together, willingly and well. Even Jocko had to learn how to convince his SEAL team to work with different types of people at all different skill levels from different departments, divisions, and nationalities, even though they only wanted to work with the other top SEAL team operators.

Being able to multiply your forces is a leverage effect in business. Being able to leverage your team is the only way, in my opinion, to be able to scale. I'm blessed to have incredible people around me: my sister Gabrielle, Eugene, Rebecca Lendino, Rebecca Kobetz, Randi Spellman, Liz Cioffi, Jackie Fodiman, Jenn Sperber, Toby Danow, Crystal Cagno, Patricia Papataros, and more.

When you build the type of organization that attracts great teammates, it becomes your responsibility to become the type of organization and the life that they envisioned. You must become their greatest protector from vendors, customers, and, many times, themselves. You have to have their back the way they have your back. For the leader of an organization, this can become your greatest challenge. As Trey Taylor says, "A CEO does only three things: sets the overall strategic vision for a company, hires and retains the best people, and makes sure there's always money in the bank."[53]

This is a great synopsis of what it takes to be a CEO. One of the greatest challenges facing business leaders today is hiring and retaining the best people. In 2022 and 2023, we saw what has been termed "the great resignation." People left companies en masse in search of greener pastures. And it's possible because people have options to switch careers in a way that they never had before. Technology is democratizing work, and the gig economy is letting people live and work from all over the world. They can pick up job after job to make a living and live life more on their terms than they could in their nine-to-five.

Twenty years ago, one of the most common ways to create a nice life was to have a long-term career with a single company. Today, if you want to build a company with employees who have ten-, twenty-, and thirty-year careers with you, the only way to do it is to build an organization where you put your money where your mouth is: you live by your core values and have their backs in a way that other companies don't.

This is exactly what I've tried to do with Chart Organization, Mixology Clothing Company, and ARC. Doing what I say and having my people's back are the

---

[53] Trey Taylor, *A CEO Only Does Three Things: Finding Your Focus in the C-Suite*. A Board of Advisors Book, 2020.

greatest forms of leverage I've been able to employ. When I'm recruiting for Mixology, I'm the best promoter of the company, but I recognize that every recruiter is going to promise their company is the best company. One of the strategies that I employ when recruiting is to give prospective employees a list of current employees: new employees, office employees, and long-term retail employees. I encourage the prospective employee to call them and ask them any questions they have, unfiltered—and I don't prepare the employees for the call. All my employees know they could someday get a call, but I don't give them advance notice that they'll get a call in the next few days.

I want prospects to find out everything they want to know about working at Mixology because I want it to be a relationship that works both ways. I don't want to make promises about how great we are and then have it not meet their expectations. I tell them what I expect from them, how the company operates, and our core values.

Virtually every person I've ever interviewed has told me nothing less than they are the best employee ever. No one has ever come into an interview and said they were less than incredible, whether it was true or not. But I make sure I'm fully transparent on everything about my companies. I say, "We are not perfect by any stretch of the imagination, but if you embody our core values and treat people well, then I will always have your back."

Supporting my people is a nonnegotiable for me,

one that I hope I've lived up to. I've had to fire hundreds of people over my career, and I'm sure some of those people hate my guts and some don't wish me well. I'm sure there will be some people who see I've written another book and roll their eyes. As we talked about in the previous chapter, every time you step out and take a risk in life, you become vulnerable.

When you want to do something great, whether that's writing a book, starting a business, or making a single post on social media, get ready for a line of haters. Get ready to hear from all the people who feel like you've wronged them in the past. The only people in the world who have nobody who hates them are the people who are so timid and afraid to piss anyone off that they don't do anything.

The reason I can sleep well at night despite the haters is knowing that I have the back of everyone who embodies the core values of my family and my companies. I firmly believe that this is why, as the years have gone on, the company has become better and better and why we've been able to recruit and retain better and better people.

We have employees who have been around for more than a decade and are some of our best team members. And some of our newest hires have quickly joined them as our best performers. We were able to attract these new people because the best talent wants to be around a culture of winning and success. They want to work at a company that has their back in good times and bad.

Mixology Clothing Company

Before COVID began in January 2020, we had so much hope and optimism. Then the pandemic hit us with incredible force. When we crossed the line from December 2020 to January 2021, it was one of the strangest feelings of my career. Finishing the year felt like winning the Super Bowl or winning a championship belt. We were pushed to our absolute maximum capacity of fear and obstacles. Hundreds of thousands of other businesses failed and closed that year (a number that would surpass three million by 2024). I had to use every bit of tactical creativity I had learned over the previous decade from all the times I had failed, all the mistakes I had made, and all the knowledge I had accumulated in order to win.

Yet as we finished the year, I was immediately struck with the knowledge that we now had to do it again. We finished; we won. What now?

That's what finishing can do to you. If you're not planning for what's next, finishing can be unbelievably scary. You wanted the dream car; you had your eye on that fancy watch. Now that you've gotten it, you want the next dopamine hit. You want the next thing.

Part of becoming a good finisher is learning how to be instantly ready for what's next. You finished? Okay, let's go again. No ego, no celebration. Let's get right back to work. This is what the end of 2020 taught me.

When we went into 2021, it turned out to be our best year in business ever (up until that point). Using all the hard lessons of my career and all our battlefield experience of 2020, we were able to execute on our most ambitious plans. We hired incredible people, opened more stores, refreshed and renovated existing stores, and turned every single potential obstacle into an advantage.

Learning how to finish and begin again is an important part of finishing. It's part of what I love about jiu jitsu. When you're training and get that submission, the night's not over. You slap hands, help your training partner up, and go again. After all, just because you got the finish on that round doesn't mean your opponent isn't going to come back and get you on the next one.

Mat Chat

As you begin your journey to learning these principles, remember it can take a long time to get to where you want to go. Another adage I love says, "Most people overestimate what they can do in a year and underestimate what they can do in ten years." I've learned to appreciate the journey, work, and time it takes to flush out good ideas.

Beginning with the end in mind is a learned behavior. Very few people are born understanding this principle. You can go through life spending every day showing up, working hard, heading home, watching a little TV, falling asleep, and doing it over again the next day, never improving. Sometimes you go up a little, and sometimes you go down a little, but you stay near the status quo, a market beta return.

But when you begin to internalize the principle of beginning with the end in mind, you start to become intentional about everything you do. You start to become measured and planned to achieve your most ambitious goals. You start to make a plan of attack and envision exactly what it will take to achieve your dreams. And you find when you make an actual plan, even if it's only a few bullet points long, and start to hold yourself accountable for what it takes to get what you want, you start making outsized alpha returns.

Once you successfully finish one goal, you'll find the process is easier to understand the second time. The more you understand, the easier it becomes to perform. You begin to build muscle memory.

You have to accept that it takes time to develop these instincts. It takes time to develop muscle memory. **It takes time to understand the difference between pulling a punch and yoyu (critical margin), the decision to finish, the decision to win.** It takes deep study in order to understand how to start finishing and use leverage in order to grow and scale.

Finishing tactics are about using a system of learning to develop and hone your killer instinct. The IBJJF encourages people to create a style of fighting that games the rules rather than finishes the fight. This is an incredible metaphor for the business world (and life in general). Government and bureaucracy of any kind, even if good-intentioned, create a mechanism for participants to find an edge by using the rules to win. While the rules define your objective, you should always be fighting for a finish. After all, no one goes into the Super Bowl wanting to do anything other than win—and win decisively.

Many of us have subconscious fear holding us

back, and we need to develop our skills and learn how to effectively use leverage in order to finish, whether that's closing a deal, winning a fight, or even marrying the person of our dreams.

It should be clear by now that "when you're green, you grow; when you're ripe, you rot." Once you finish, if you have embraced shoshin, a beginner's mind, you will be ready for what's next: scale and more growth.

Chapter 13
Scale and Growth

BJJ Fanatics is an online content-on-demand company that sells instructional videos made by the biggest names in grappling (such as Gordon Ryan and John Danaher). When BJJ Fanatics was founded by BJJ enthusiast and businessman Michael Zenga and multiple-time jiu jitsu world champion Bernardo Ferreira, there were other jiu jitsu content and video companies already in the market, many of which had existed for years.

When building a business in a niche market, you're typically not expecting to become the next Amazon. You're fully aware it's in a niche. I wrote this book for a specific subset of people, for instance. You build a niche business because you love that niche. When Michael, a talented internet-focused businessperson, partnered with Bernardo, a world champion, they set about building their business with a good heart.

Today, they've built a phenomenal, world-class business, one that's been able to scale beyond expectations. Why? It has a lot to do with their character and their dedication to what I call the three keys to success: show up, follow up, and don't give up.

Jiu Jitsu Principle: Continuous Improvement

In a 2017 Instagram post after his first ADCC championship win, Gordon Ryan gave fans some advice:

> If there's a lesson to be learned. It is that no matter how good you are. No matter what you achieve. Never believe your own hype. Show up to training every single fucking day like you ain't shit. Even after everything I did. I didn't take double gold. And the matches I won were not all by submission. Remember these words. And you too can accomplish what I have. And possible far more.[54]

This is an amazing metaphor for scale and growth. I often share this quote with my team when we do something great. (I also often say it to myself.) As my sensei has told us over the years, jiu jitsu is a jealous mistress. You can train every day for years, work on your technique, watch videos, take notes, drill, and

---

[54] Gordon Ryan (@gordonlovesjiujitsu), "Ahhh. So much to say," Instagram photo, September 24, 2017, https://www.instagram.com/p/BZb45qThfvK/.

cross-train, but as soon as you go on a one-week vacation, eating and drinking yourself silly, much of that work will quickly evaporate. Your knowledge might not be perishable, but your ability to execute on that knowledge is.

It takes constant and consistent dedication to jiu jitsu to maintain a high level of skill. The same principle applies to business. The only difference is it's easier to call yourself out in jiu jitsu because your opponents and teammates will expose every single weakness.

In business, you can hide. You can hide behind your desk (instead of networking or going to an event), a Zoom call (when a handshake would have sealed the deal), or a coworker (when you should have been the one there). It's easy to surround yourself with busywork: "I need to make these phone calls." "I have to clean my desk." "I need to review these reports."

While these tasks have a purpose, don't lose sight of what drives the business forward. If you want scale and growth moments, you have to continuously remind yourself to refocus on the most important aspects of your business.

In jiu jitsu, there is almost nowhere to hide. Every night when you show up, your teammates will know exactly where you are in the pecking order because at the start and end of every class, students are lined up by rank. Black belts typically face the rest of the academy, and across, the line starts with brown belts and continues down to white belts. Even within each belt, students are often ranked by up to four stripes.

Several times in this book we've talked about the

blue belt blues and how it feels when other students start passing you by. One of the ways this passage happens is because you find little places to hide and never reach the scale and growth moments, such as avoiding certain teammates, sitting out on drills, showing up late, missing warmups, skipping cross-training sessions, ignoring your diet, forgetting to stretch, and the list goes on. Instead of seizing opportunities, you stay in your comfort zone and plateau. In order to get to the next level, you have to take a risk or jump into action like my brother-in-law, Jared, did for Mixology during COVID lockdowns, Michael and Bernardo did with BJJ Fanatics, or Gordon did when he won his first ADCC title.

What Happens When You Achieve Success

Remember the *Business Jiu Jitsu* logo? It's a Zen symbol called an ensō. The ensō represents the oneness of life, the spirit of harmonious cooperation, refinement of character, the visible and invincible, absolute fullness and emptiness, and endlessness. It's a pattern represented in cultures all over the world, all of whom understand that the beginning and the end are deeply intertwined.

When you've won, that's not the end. It's simply the starting point of something new. In order to continue to grow, you follow the same cycle. The fear can be overwhelming, knowing that you worked so hard to get to the finish line and now you have to get up and do it all over again.

It's hard to stay on top. It's hard to maintain a career. It's hard to keep building a business. And as you keep building that business, you have more employees, more responsibilities, and bigger decisions. The weight can be difficult to carry.

Then, you get through a difficult season, like the Great Recession or Hurricane Sandy or COVID, and find success, only to realize that you have to do it all over again. Or, even harder, you lose, and you have to find the strength to get back up and try again.

My dad often says that quitting and getting fired are the same thing. In this case, winning and losing are the same thing. You've come to the end of something—a month, a quarter, a fight, a deal—and now you're faced with what comes next. Win or lose, you have to find the will to continue and the courage to grow.

Professional athletes have to train and prepare for each new fight. As they do, they are forced to evolve. The more they grow, the more fights they win. When they get to the moment of spotlight and a belt is wrapped around their waist, they have to ask themselves: now what?

The answer to that question is how you keep pushing yourself to get to the next level. Jiu jitsu can be monotonous. You learn techniques. You practice the techniques. You spar to test the techniques. As we talked about in Chapter 5, sometimes it can feel like you're standing still, especially if you're in a group of people who are progressing at roughly the same pace you are.

This is why competing is so important. It lets you

see your skill level benchmarked against other people. Jiu jitsu is an individual competition, but you need teammates in order to train and get better. More specifically, you need to spar with teammates of all skill levels in order to scale and grow.

Most importantly, you need to have what Eastern philosophy calls shoshin, or the beginner's mind. A beginner's mind is the willingness to admit you don't know everything and learn something new. My sensei reminds us to have hibi shoshin or an everyday beginner's mind, meaning that every day when you show up, you have to show up ready to learn, ready to grow, and ready to scale.

Business Principle: Small Goals for Large Growth

As an entrepreneur, you're expected to be good at everything. You need to develop many skills, including hiring, managing, selling, payroll, law, marketing, social media, tax, etc. The list is never-ending. But once you master one area, for example in social media marketing like Instagram, it becomes irrelevant, so you move on to TikTok. Wait, that's owned by the Chinese government. Better start a Pinterest. No, YouTube's the place to be...just kidding. Have you heard Twitter is back? Oops, it's called X now.

How are you supposed to master all these different things? The truth is you probably can't. However, you can practice kaizen, which is the idea that you only need to get a little bit better every day. As jiu jitsu teaches us, no matter what comes at you, it's important to stay malleable enough to keep moving, keep trying, and keep learning the best you can, day after day. This desire and consistency to get a little bit better every day is the essence of how to reach the next level.

People who are unaware of how kaizen helps them achieve large goals can sometimes find it difficult to stay the course. Maybe they recently achieved a large goal (or experienced a bad loss) or are stuck in place and trying to break free. Either way, the solution is the same: set small, achievable goals. Moving from purple belt to brown belt can take years. To keep your momentum over a long period of time, it helps to set small goals for yourself that can be done in several days or weeks. This works whether you focus on fitness, health, or work projects.

Whenever I want to improve my jiu jitsu practice but don't have the bandwidth to sign up for a tournament (remember, competition is a cheat code to rapid improvement), I choose a new fitness goal. One goal I return to is running a 5k race, though there are many types of small, achievable goals.

The act of training for that race increases my cardio and lights up my jiu jitsu. The race makes me goal-oriented and helps me make better decisions across all areas of my life. If you don't have small goals, it's easier to say, "Sure, I'll go out to dinner tonight." "Yeah, I'll have another beer." "We should definitely get the dessert." If you're training for a 5k, even though it's a small goal, you're not going to make those decisions.

While it's important not to lose sight of the bigger picture, after a big victory or big loss, it can help to focus on small, micro goals. As you achieve these small goals, you often find yourself making bigger progress in other areas of your life.

> Use the link in the Resources section at the back of the book to download a copy of my daily habit tracker.

When you have a long-term goal and you show up every day thinking you're getting a little better but you're not seeing the growth or improvement you want, it can be frustrating. But when you set a short-term goal for yourself, you often experience a major growth spurt. It may seem surprising—"All I did was train for a 5k!"—but it's not only about the training. It's about all the good decisions you make on a daily basis to meet that short-term goal.

At first glance, kaizen seems to be in contrast to the idea of scale. People often think of scale and growth as hyper-scaling growth. And it's true: big audacious goals and big audacious risks can get you to the next level.

However, if you've been living your life in accordance with the principles of kaizen, getting a little bit better day after day over a long period of time, when the moment comes to take that big audacious risk, you'll be ready. In fact, you won't be taking as big of a risk as it seems to the outside world because you've been putting in this almost invisible work.

Often people don't understand that even small goals like training for a 5k can affect every decision in your life. You get up early to run before work, so you get to work on time. "Well, since I'm here on time, I might as well eat a healthy breakfast." "Well, I'm already here on time and I've eaten a healthy breakfast, so I might as well do all my work." Every single decision compounds on itself. Before you realize it, you've accomplished much more than you set out to do.

As you begin to incorporate the principle of kaizen into your life, you may find that you learn more. In jiu jitsu, we talk about the same concepts and techniques year in and year out. If you approach each lesson with fresh eyes, you'll find your understanding gets deeper with each repetition. Harder, however, is maintaining the beginner's mind when you experience a loss. Sometimes, when a person spars and is completely dominated, they walk out with excuses and anger dripping from their tongue. Contrast that with people who practice shoshin and lose; they think, "Yes! More to learn!" They know the more people you train with, the more you get to learn and understand.

Find the Root Issue

Throughout the course of this book, you've heard me talk about having to furlough employees and make the decision to not pay millions of dollars of rent and other expenses. It's easy to skim over these sentences and not feel the pain and fear associated with making these decisions or the weight that came with them.

Brian Sanders was one of the people I had to furlough at the beginning of COVID. He managed our shipping and receiving department in our warehouse, but we weren't receiving inventory or shipping inventory to stores, which meant his department was shut down. When I made the gut-wrenching call to let him know that I didn't know when or if I would be able to rehire him, his response blew me away: "Jordan, I'm with you, no matter what. My wife and I can withstand this, whether it's a couple of weeks or a couple of months. I don't want you to feel any pressure from me. If you need anything, whatever it is, I'm still here for you."

This was one in a series of calls that were some of the hardest I have ever had to make, and it was a beautiful thing to hear. In the terrifying first days of COVID, Brian made me feel that Mixology Clothing Company was going to make it through. And when the business began to ramp up again after quarantine ended, he was one of the first people I brought back from furlough.

As we moved into the summer of 2021, business didn't simply ramp up—it ramped and ramped and ramped. We were opening three new stores. Sales were increasing. Mixology was growing rapidly.

One day, Brian walked into my office. We had recently moved into a new warehouse space because we had outgrown our previous warehouse, and he said, "The drivers are at their absolute wit's end. They're driving all over the tri-state area. They're driving from the Hamptons, New York, out to Livingston, New

Jersey, and there's a four-hour difference between those two places."

At this point, the new stores had opened, and the old stores had reopened; the new hires were excelling, and business was booming. In fact, the business was bigger than it had been when we closed. We went from navigating shrinking pains to staying in business to growing pains. The strategic risks we made had paid off, except our business wasn't set up to support these new stores. Brian now had the same number of drivers and the same number of trucks but more stores on the route and more inventory coming in. By the time he came to me, he was immensely stressed. The drivers were beginning to break under the weight of our growth. They were at each other's throats, at Brian's throat, and at their families' throats.

Despite the upturn in business, we were still trying to be exceptionally careful in our investment decisions, and my employees were making sure to have my back. They were being careful not to spend frivolous money and keeping costs as low as possible. It never occurred to him that the problem would be easy to solve by purchasing another van and hiring another driver (a few more of each, actually). Brian's thought process was, *If I get another van and hire another person, we'll be above budget.* He didn't realize that budgets change when you're growing a business.

One reason many businesses fail is because they don't devote enough resources to growth. They worry about wasting money when spending that money would actually be an investment in their business. (Have you ever checked out at a retail store, and their computer appears to be running DOS or Windows 95? It's not nearly as good of an experience as checking out with Square or Shopify.)

I listened to Brian, and said, "I don't think we have a driver problem. I think we have an understaffing problem. We need to buy more vans, and we need to hire more drivers."

I explained to Brian that he was still in COVID mindset—still on defense. It was time for us to go on the offense. We had made it through the problems, taken risks, built three new stores, and bought and opened a new warehouse. All of these signaled the beginning of scale, our next phase.

We bought a few more trucks and hired a few more drivers, and the problems that were causing the business stress were solved. These moments of uncomfortable growth happen every single day in business. Ask yourself: are you curing the symptoms, or are you getting to the root cause?

For example, say your house is being overrun with rodents and bugs. Your first instinct may be to call the exterminator because you don't notice that you're living in a mess: dirty dishes overflowing in the sink, pizza boxes piled up in the corner, old drink cans and bottles cluttering every table. Should you call the exterminator, or should you clean your house? You may need to call that exterminator, but first, you have to clean the mess. Otherwise, the bugs and rodents will keep coming back.

The same analysis should happen when we get sick. Yes, you need to get some medicine to handle the current illness, but you also need to ask yourself how you got there in the first place. Have you been burning the candle at both ends? Have you been getting enough sleep? Have you been drinking too much or consuming an unhealthy diet?

It is a rare person who can diagnose their own metaphorical dirty house problem. Rather, they're battling the symptoms. Only the most introspective people can think about their own problems. It's far easier to see the root cause of other people's problems.

The goal is to ensure you dig down to the root cause of every issue that crops up as you begin to grow and scale. It will feel uncomfortable, but growth is located on the other side of our comfort zone. With Brian, the issue was our drivers were overstressed. Instead of finding a Band-Aid solution, I dug deeper and found that we had the same number of drivers as we did when the business was 50 percent smaller. If you can begin to filter your thinking through this lens, you can start to make decisions that solve problems quickly, and scale is sure to follow.

Mat Chat

On November 20, 2020, I came home from training and, as usual, sat down to write notes about that night's training. I started to jot down notes about my sensei's mat chat, as I've done hundreds of times before:

> Sensei's mat chat: LOL. It was amazing, and I already forgot it. He mentioned "becoming the book." He mentioned countless techniques. He also mentioned something about Kazaa and Eddie Vedder. I can't remember what.

I knew it was a great story, but I couldn't remember the details. Then, three years later, Sensei Nardu started telling the story again in a mat chat. I was so excited to finally learn about it. The story was about finding a song.

Back in the 2000s, my sensei heard a song on the radio that he really liked, and he wanted to download it using Kazaa, a peer-to-peer file-sharing software (similar to Napster). Back then, you couldn't just look up the list of music played on a station through their website. He finally figured out the name of the song, opened Kazaa to download the song, and realized he had already downloaded it.

This is a perfect metaphor for what most of us do in life. We are thirsty for knowledge, so we read lots of books, listen to podcasts, talk to mentors, and work in our business only to find the knowledge we need was there the whole time. You ask a question and, upon hearing the answer, realize you learned it long ago. As the Alchemist tells Santiago when he wants to learn the secrets of alchemy in *The Alchemist*, "There is one way to learn. It's through action. Everything you need to know you have learned through your journey. You need to learn only one thing more."

The irony of learning the story a second time was not lost on me. The first time I heard it, I had forgotten the core insight by the end of the story. However, the second time I heard it, almost three years later, the message hit me like a bolt of lightning. How many of life's lessons do we have to keep repeating and learning in order for them to sink in and become a true part of our memory?

Each time you come to a moment of transformation and alchemy in your life, jiu jitsu, or business, in order to get to the next level, sometimes you have to go back to the beginning: the most fundamental aspects of what you've learned. Often, you'll find that you've already learned them, but the relearning gives you a deeper understanding. This is why I've taken accounting classes three times. This is why my sensei repeats mat chats every few years and why I continue to retell important stories, lessons, and anecdotes from my life to my teams and on my podcast. I am simultaneously teaching the lessons to others and reinforcing them with myself.

As you look to scale and grow to the next level, it's important to remember what you did to become successful in the first place: running, eating well, reading, being kind to your family, treating your employees well, etc. It's common to focus on these fundamentals for a time and then, as you try new techniques, forget about the little things that set up the launchpad to get you where you are.

You see this happen with celebrities. They work hard, move to Hollywood, get their big break, and then experience a downward spiral. Think of Robert Downey Jr. He reached the pinnacle of success and then had a fall from grace. Luckily for him, he was able to completely revitalize his career by first recognizing the bad habits and bad behaviors and then refocusing on the things that brought him success in the first place. By combining a refocus on his fundamentals with his natural talents, he was again able to rise to the top and is one of the most successful actors in Hollywood. (Sadly and unfortunately, RDJ is the exception, not the rule. Most don't recover; they wash out and burn out.)

It's crucial that you don't forget where you started and what made you successful as you grow. Because as you grow, you'll find that people start to tell you how great you are. They'll put you on a pedestal. You see big money in the bank and your name in headlines. All of these can cause your ego to explode.

All of these business skills that lead to success, like jiu jitsu skills, are perishable. One week of bad habits can interrupt your growth.

In order to get to the biggest moments of growth and scale, it's important to recognize what habits help you get to where you are and keep them up every day. If you're going on vacation, go on vacation with intention. Find a place to train every morning. Schedule time each day to work on a business project that you haven't had time to focus on. Bring those three books you've been meaning to read. Bring your journal to think through that idea that's been in the back of your mind. I've had some of my biggest breakthrough moments on vacations when I leave for the trip with the right intentions.

It's equally important to ensure you don't let obstacles knock you off your habits. There are always going to be setbacks. Sometimes the journey takes us right back to the beginning. Too often people see adversity as holding them back. These are usually the people who give up as soon as they run into obstacles. The strongest people use adversity as a launching point.

Ultimately, this book is about the hundreds of thousands of decisions I made early in my career and how I used the lessons I absorbed from each of those decisions—both good and bad—to know what to do when a potential disaster hit. When you start to get success, it can feel exasperating or intoxicating to do it all over again. But that's what life is: an endless cycle of putting yourself out there and starting anew. Like the ensō, you end at the beginning.

Conclusion

In 2017, Mixology Clothing Company was evolving. We were transitioning from a small mom-and-pop business to a medium-sized business. It quickly became clear to me that, as the company became bigger, I needed to create a training program so I could communicate the simple messages and core values of the business down to even the most junior employee.

There's a business joke I love:

> The top monkey on the tree, the CEO, looks down, and all he sees is smiles, but the bottom monkey, the most junior employee, looks up...and all they see is assholes.

This is such a simple and clear metaphor for the problems found in so many organizations and teams.

Your job as the CEO is to make sure this is not your company. And it is unbelievably hard, especially as you grow. Why? Because when you found a business as a passionate entrepreneur or creator, you know every employee (and most of your customers) by name. As you grow, you open a second location and then a third, and by the time you get to the fifth location, you realize you don't know everyone anymore. You don't know every customer. And all the little things you did on a daily basis to make the business a success are not being communicated to the average employee. The culture falls apart, and the business begins to shrink back to one or two locations, and you're left trying to figure out what went wrong.

One of the benefits that I had going into the fashion retail business was that I didn't know much about fashion or retail, so I came into it with a different approach to team building and business growth. I put more emphasis on core values than teaching my employees about fashion. I knew that if I hired people who were obsessed with fashion and loved selling, I could teach them what they needed to know about teamwork, leadership, and business fundamentals and let them be the experts in fashion.

Even when you think you've mastered something, be open to learning more. In *Turn the Ship Around!*, David Marquet talks about his training to captain a new class of submarine.[55] He was given an absurdly large manual that covered how every single system on the ship worked—and he learned every single page. Then, right before he was deployed, the Navy reassigned him to a submarine class he knew nothing about.

He had to rely completely on his team. Instead of being able to lead using his knowledge of the systems,

---

[55] L. David Marquet, Turn the Ship Around!: A True Story of Turning Followers into Leaders (Penguin: New York, 2012).

he had to lead by managing the people who had the knowledge. He had to embrace a beginner's mind in order to learn all the different aspects of the ship from the people who were now the experts.

In 2017, as we were going through this growth, I came up with an idea that I immediately wrote down in my notebook: Fashion 101, a training program to communicate simple ideas to the whole staff so they do things the way that I would do them. I sat on this idea for a while and then shared it with my executive team.

The response was a lot of eye rolling and comments such as, "That's a stupid name," "That's a stupid idea," and "I don't think that'll work." As an entrepreneur, you'd better get used to hearing these types of comments from the closest people in your life. As we talked about in Chapter 6, sometimes your partners, friends, and family root for you, and sometimes they're your biggest detractors.

But when you know your business, you see a problem, and you create an initiative or program to solve it, don't let a name stop you. You can always change a name. I knew I needed to communicate these ideas, so I began writing Fashion 101 on the heels of COVID. As we entered 2021, Fashion 101 turned into Mix University (Mix U, for short), which became the foundation for something beyond a simple training program.

I was blessed to have two incredible partners in the creation of Agile Retail Company (ARC): Abdaal Mazhar Shafi and Arya Sajedi. Abdaal, in addition to partnering with me at ARC, also started an incredible nonprofit called UpstartED, whose mission is to transform the mental health and educational and employment outcomes of children and teens through technical and entrepreneurial programs. For me and Mix U, this meant he had an incredible knowledge base on how to build a training program. He saved us years of trial and error in building Mix U to become something incredible.

Together with Abdaal and Becca Lendino, one of my executives, we began to outline the curriculum for Mix U with the intention of putting our entire junior staff through an eight-week leadership training seminar in the summer of 2021. As we launched the program, I told my executive team that the real goal of the program was to be able to recruit great talent so we could retain more of our junior employees, and they would want to build careers at Mixology and consider us a desirable place to find growth and opportunity in place of or after college.

In 2023, it's ubiquitous to hear, "You can never find anyone to work." A few years before, there was a never-ending news cycle with terms like, "The Great Resignation." Unlike many other companies, Mixology never had trouble finding people who wanted to work with us. When people asked me how I found team members, I explained, "I have an internal company training program with hundreds of people participating. We can cherry-pick the best participants from the program."

In that first summer, over one hundred forty of our

junior employees signed up to participate. We even had several customers who paid to join the program. When I first said to my executive team, "Let's sell this to our customers too. Why wouldn't they be interested in fashion and leadership?" the reaction was poor at best.

However, I've found that every time you tell someone you want to do something, no matter what it is, they're going to tell you you're wrong. Jamie Giovinazzo experienced the same pushback when he started his meal prep business, Eat Clean Bro.[56] All of his friends told him that he couldn't call his business Eat Clean Bro, that it would be a terrible business name. His dad finally told him, "That's who you are. Just be who you are, and you'll do great." Now Eat Clean Bro is a major success endorsed by several celebrities.

Jamie told me, "Jordan, back in the day, if I had told my friends I was going to the moon, they would say, 'You're an idiot. You'll never get there.' Today, if I told them I was going to the moon, they'd ask, 'How are you going to get there?'" Jamie learned, as I have, that after you have success, people start to listen to you in a whole different way—usually. Sometimes, you have to prove yourself over and over again.

With Mix U, as the eight weeks came to a close, I knew it had been a massive success. One reason was the additional step we took at the end of the program.

---

[56] Ep 43: Jamie Giovinazzo | Overcoming Adversity & Becoming a Household Name

When you finish taking a program at Harvard Business School Online, they give you instructions on how to list and link the program on your LinkedIn page and resume. I loved the idea, so at the end of Mix U, I gave all the students instructions on how to list it on their LinkedIn as well as on their resumes. This meant that when they were going out and looking for jobs, they could show that they participated in our leadership program. I also told them they could use me and my team as a reference.

This willingness to support someone even when they're not working at Mixology is something I do for every employee. When you work for Mixology, whether for an internship, co-op, part time, or full time, and you decide to leave, you leave knowing that I'm going to be your biggest supporter. If someone calls me as a reference, I'm going to be your biggest raving fan.

Having this attitude has brought back several incredible employees. Becca Lendino, for example, started at Mixology when she was seventeen years old. She eventually left to work at Macy's, but during COVID, they furloughed her, and she came back to Mixology (another one of my big hiring risks), where she immediately made a massive positive impact on the business. Within a year, she was promoted to vice president, and she's now one of my key executives, effectively running our retail operations along with being a buyer and wearing many other hats. Becca was also instrumental in the continued development of Mix U and incorporated learnings from her career into the program.

When we finished the first iteration of Mix U, I was ready to get back on the mat for the next round. Starting in early 2022, we began hosting one-hour seminars throughout the year, which we called "Mix U Presents," on a variety of topics. One month we did Mix U Presents Health and Wellness. Another month we did Mix U Presents Personal Finance. For that seminar, the CEO and founder of the Acorn Investing app, Walter Cruttenden, came in and spoke to my company, along with a few hundred family, friends, and vendors, about personal finance.

Every time we hosted a seminar, I felt a little more gratified. But the biggest gratification came in early 2022 when something incredible happened. We began to receive resumes for our summer internship program at a rate we had never seen before. And guess what was listed on many of those resumes. The Mix U eight-week leadership program from the previous summer. Seeing this, the team developed an in-house recruiting mechanism to find our best front-line junior retail employees and give them an opportunity to build careers at Mixology.

So many people think fashion is full of people brimming with confidence and poise. It couldn't be further from the truth. Fashion is actually a place of misfits who are trying to find their voices. I'm proud that Mixology has become a place where many of our best people were able to find their voices. Fashion is, after all, a way of being able to tell the world who you are without having to say a word. Many women who started with us as shy teenagers are now in their mid-to late-thirties and running departments and stores. Mix U is a way to continue providing women with a place to grow.

Three years later, Mix U has become a smashing success. We've had over a thousand people go through the program. Three years in a row we've recruited better talent than we've ever been able to recruit before. Mix U, a program that was almost laughed out of the organization a few years before, now has other companies looking to buy and invest in this training program so they can have it at their company too.

It's important to realize that when you start something new, many people won't understand. They won't get it because they don't know how to begin with the end in mind. While I didn't know exactly what this program would turn into when I started it, I did see the problem I had to solve, and I knew that I wanted the finish to ensure that every employee was inspired to treat our customers as I would treat them (i.e., when they looked up, they wouldn't see just assholes).

When we received the avalanche of resumes for our internship program, I knew that was my finishing moment. I had seen my idea through to the end, but I also knew it was the very beginning again. We've since been working to make the program larger by leveraging the talents of even more people on my team, including many alumni of Mix U who now run the program.

Aim for Success

I've often found that when people tell their story, it's

the story of only their successes. I wanted to tell my story differently. After all, I started my career in the 2008 Great Recession. Hurricane Sandy almost destroyed Mixology Clothing Company in 2012. My failed manufacturing business lost us $1 million in 2015. We struggled through COVID in 2020.

I have also had successes. We survived COVID and came out stronger than we could have ever imagined. We created and launched ARC. I've invested in companies, bought buildings, raised tens of millions of dollars, sold well over $150 million of clothing and accessories, closed deals, negotiated hundreds of commercial leases, built dozens of stores for myself and tenants, flipped homes, sold toner, flipped omelets, MCe'd bar mitzvahs, caddied, and the list goes on.

If you look at my life in total, I have had more success than failure. However, my successes are made up of failures experienced on a daily basis. Each failure has been an investment in loss—tuition payments—propelling me to new heights. I may have tapped one million times in the dojo during practice, but those taps led to me winning at the critical moment when it matters.

However, the truth is the next crisis is always around the corner. I may not know what that crisis will be, but I do know there will be one. The question becomes how do you wake up with optimism no matter what the future holds?

You can't predict what a crisis will look like. But you can be ready to respond and adapt. That's what business jiu jitsu is: the ability to adapt to any circumstance, good or bad.

Any time I need to vent, and I bring some problem or obstacle to my dad, he gives me the same answer: **"Don't you mean opportunity?"**

Business jiu jitsu is about seizing the opportunities as they come and using the obstacles as launching pads to success. It's building your muscle memory through continuous learning and the creation of healthy habits (healthy for your body, mind, soul...and business).

So many businesses fold in their first ten years. How do you defy the odds? How do you take that risk when so many other people can't?

You use the tools and techniques shared in this book.

Here is my simple formula:

1. Show up.
2. Follow up.
3. Don't give up.

If I can do it, you can do it. I am as regular as it gets. I don't have any special abilities. I don't have any special gifts. I boast average intelligence and average athleticism. My only gift is that I keep showing up and refuse to give up.

What will you accomplish when you show up, follow up, and refuse to give up?

It Couldn't Be Done
By Edgar Albert Guest

Somebody said that it couldn't be done
But he with a chuckle replied
That "maybe it couldn't," but he would be one
Who wouldn't say so till he'd tried.
So he buckled right in with the trace of a grin
On his face. If he worried he hid it.
He started to sing as he tackled the thing
That couldn't be done, and he did it!

Somebody scoffed: "Oh, you'll never do that;
At least no one ever has done it;"
But he took off his coat and he took off his hat
And the first thing we knew he'd begun it.
With a lift of his chin and a bit of a grin,
Without any doubting or quiddit,
He started to sing as he tackled the thing
That couldn't be done, and he did it.

There are thousands to tell you it cannot be done,
There are thousands to prophesy failure,
There are thousands to point out to you one by one,
The dangers that wait to assail you.
But just buckle in with a bit of a grin,
Just take off your coat and go to it;
Just start in to sing as you tackle the thing
That "cannot be done," and you'll do it.

Resources

The habit tracker on the following two pages is similar to what I use to hold myself accountable toward my goals. As I refer it throughout the day, I apply the following keys to represent my progress on each task:

X = not done
● = worked on
✓ = completed
– = pushing out

For the exercise portion:

C = cardio
CT = cross training
N = no gi
G = gi

You can create your own habit tracker or go to www.businessjiujitsu.com/tracker to get a blank one I've created with the jiu jitsu community in mind.

TO DO:

DAILY	M	T	W	TH	F	S	SU
Eat healthy							
Intermittent fast							
Drink water—take vitamins							
Read							
Pray – Daily Stoic							
BJJ Book – Lisa							
BJJ Podcast – ck in with VA							
Content							
BJJ – Train							
Cardio / Cross Train							

2024 ACTION PLAN

WEEKLY FOLLOW UP	M	T	W	TH	F	NOTES
ARC						
PE Investments						
Property Managers						
Leasing Agents						
Contractors						
Mix U + Fashion 1st Responders						
Advertising						
Loans/Refi (see schedule)						
Monthly/Weekly Reports						
Vacancy/Rent Rolls						

Properties	!	M	T	W	TH	F	NOTES
Flips							
Mixology Properties							
Colorado							
Florida							
North Carolina							
Pennsylvania							
Texas #1							
Texas #2							

NEW IDEAS

HOUSE PROJECTS

WEEK: **Q:** **DATE:**

PROJECTS	!	M	T	W	TH	F	NOTES
New store – Florida							
Texas refi							
Store refresh – NJ							
Lease renewal							
PROJECTS HOLD							
Roof project - PA							

Leads	!	M	T	W	TH	F	NOTES
Coffee shop – TX							
Dollar Store – PA							
Supermarket - PA							

Tasks	!	M	T	W	TH	F	NOTES
Call publisher re book cover							
Set up team dinner – NYC							
Draft investor letter – Q2 report							
Lunch with Mom							

PLANS	!	M	T	W	TH	F	NOTES
Plan property visit – PA (Sept)							

SANDBOX

Acknowledgments

This book, much like my journey in jiu jitsu, has been both immensely rewarding and incredibly challenging, pushing me to grow in ways I never anticipated. When I set out to write it, I knew exactly what I wanted it to be about: how the principles of jiu jitsu have transcended the sport to help me in so many other areas of my life, particularly with the pressure and intensity of being an entrepreneur.

I could never have imagined how rewarding it would be to begin conversations with so many project stakeholders on social media and, ultimately, through my podcast. Talking to some of my heroes and the world's most accomplished athletes, coaches, and more has been an incredible experience.

I want to start by giving some personal acknowledgments and also share some of my favorite conversations on the podcast.

First and foremost, I thank my father, Glenn, who has been my greatest mentor. He has led with his actions and allowed me to carve my way, always letting me figure it out in my own time. He often says that people do things when they're ready, not when others want them to, and I have found that to be incredibly accurate both as a father and as a business owner.

I also want to acknowledge my mother, Lisa, and my siblings, Gabrielle and Tyler, whose unwavering support and love have been a constant source of strength and inspiration throughout my life.

To my Sensei Nardu Debrah: Sensei, you have devoted yourself to the arts—both martial arts and fine arts. Your dedication and passion have been a beacon of inspiration to me. You once said something incredibly profound that has stayed with me: "Become the book." As someone who loves to read and learn, this call to action has been a powerful reminder to take what I am learning and use it, not to let it sit dormant in my mind. Too many people in the world have wonderful ideas and know exactly what to do but never take action. They watch as people around them, who are less smart, less talented, and less hungry, go out and win simply by taking action. "Become the book" has become a rallying call for me, often scribbled in my journals and on the pages of my favorite books when I revisit them years later. Thank you, Sensei Nardu, for instilling this drive for action inside of me.

I want to extend my deepest gratitude to Abdaal Mazhar Shafi. Abdaal, you read the entire book, proofread it, and gleaned the most important insights in just a few days. Your ability to pick out your favorite quotes and provide a deep understanding of the book is appreciated beyond measure. Your intellect and enthusiasm are inspiring. You are not only an incredible friend and business partner but also a massive resource to our business ARC and my work at Business Jiu-Jitsu, Mixology Clothing Company, and Chart Organization. I also want to acknowledge your crucial role in the early days of Mix U. Your inspiration and experiences at UpstartEd were instrumental in helping me launch it. Thank you for your unwavering support and for believing in this project as much as I do.

Next, my team. Everything that I do in my life and career is a reflection of my team. It would be impossible for me to run multiple businesses without leveraging the talent and hard work of hundreds of people reporting to me. Many of the lessons in this book and the stories from my past are the hard-fought battles of learning how to be an effective leader and make good decisions. Unfortunately, many of those good decisions came at the expense of bad decisions earlier in my career. My team often picked up my slack and carried the weight, and I am incredibly grateful to call these amazing people my friends and associates. I'm eternally grateful for all their hard work and for putting their trust in me over these past few decades. Without their trust, all of my ideas would simply be lost in the ether. Thank you to the amazing people at Chart Organization, Mixology Clothing Company, Agile Retail Company, and all of our portfolio companies for making what I do look much easier. The number one question I get asked by new and aspiring entrepreneurs is, "Isn't it hard to find good people?" While I agree it's hard to find people, if you internalize the messages of this book, learn from your mistakes, and build exceptional core values of honesty and integrity, then you too can build a great team. It's all about how you treat people, whether in your company or at home.

I also want to acknowledge Mike Rogers, the CEO of Critical Response Group (CRG). Mike has been a student of my father, Glenn, who seeded his business when it was simply an idea around the kitchen table. Mike is a high performer and an incredible human, and it has been a privilege to invest in his company and watch him grow. He went from being the student to becoming the teacher, and I can't describe the satisfaction I have received from being a small part of his story. I am so grateful he came on the podcast and shared his thoughts, and I look forward to many more years of friendship, conversations, and business together. I also want to commend him for the relationship he has built with my father. Many entrepreneurs and people come to my father for advice, knowing he has been successful across many decades and industries. It's a shame how many of those people don't take his advice, finding that good advice is sometimes the hardest to hear and implement. It has been an honor to watch Mike implement my father's suggestions, advice, and knowledge, helping him win in business. It's certainly only a small part of Mike's framework and mentorship, but watching little bits of my father's DNA make someone else successful has been incredibly rewarding. Thank you, Mike.

When I began this project, I wrote down a list of some of the best coaches and athletes in the world, and two of those names were Gordon Ryan and John Danaher. I didn't know them well, having only met them in training at the Renzo Gracie Academy as one of the many faces in the class, but the conversations on the podcast with them and the attention on social media they helped garner, led to many more conversations with world champions, billionaires, CEOs, Navy SEALs, special operators, and other incredible people adjacent to the jiu jitsu world. Their support validated the project in many ways and lent legitimacy to my desire to explore these topics with the best. Often, taking a risk on an unknown can have the opposite of the intended effect. I hope my work and conversations have honored their belief in me, and that this book represents their philosophy in teaching and action on the mat. There is no doubt that Gordon's accomplishments in the modern jiu-jitsu age have helped push the sport forward, and John's teachings have been a massive part of both Gordon's athletic pursuits and certainly my business pursuits.

I would also like to recognize Mo Jassim, the lead organizer for the ADCC Abu Dhabi Combat Club, and one of my real estate business partners, Kenny Blatt. When the Danaher Death Squad moved to Puerto Rico, I noticed they were hanging out at the Ritz Carlton Reserve property there, which Kenny developed. I asked Kenny if he knew about these large, musclebound, tattooed jiu-jitsu fighters, and he said he was aware and connected me with Mo. When I asked Mo to be on the podcast, he instantaneously and without hesitation brought Gordon Ryan onto an email thread. I tried to reciprocate, but Mo wouldn't have it. He didn't want or ask for anything, was only willing to help me in my pursuit of researching this book. I will be eternally grateful as I see him as a catalyst for helping me move this project in the right direction.

JP Dinnell is a former Navy SEAL who works under Jocko Willink at Echelon Front. I had the opportunity to hear JP speak at an Echelon Front training session, and his story moved me deeply. Of course, his exploits as a SEAL and task unit leader under Jocko Willink are incredibly commendable, but it is who he is as a human and the lessons of extreme ownership that he embraced in his life that helped round out the pages of this book, especially in Chapter 6, which I view as the most important chapter about family and friends. It's tough to overcome the challenges of divorce, in his case multiple times, and realize that you are, in fact, the center of all your problems and that no one else is. You have the ability to change your circumstances by becoming the main character of your own book, your own movie, and taking responsibility for everything you say and do, never blaming anybody else for your misfortune. No one else articulated that as well as JP did when I heard him speak, and for that, I am incredibly grateful. I am also exceptionally grateful for his coming on the podcast and sharing his story.

I want to give a big shoutout and thank you to a mentor, coach, and friend, Richard Byrne. Rich's list of accomplishments is great, both in the business and the jiu-jitsu world. What stands out most to me is his dedication and consistency in life. He shows up every day, over and over again, consistently training and consistently working hard. Throughout the years, he has taught me much about jiu-jitsu and what it takes to compete in the business world at the highest levels. Not by any single conversation we've had about business, but by how he shows up for his students and trains at 5 a.m. every weekend, whether there's one student or twenty on the mats. There is no excuse for not making time for the things in your life that matter, and Rich, while running some of the biggest companies in the world, always makes time for his family, his students, and his businesses. Thank you for many years of wisdom, excellent teaching, and the many books you passed to me, which have impacted me significantly.

One of the special relationships I've formed from this podcast is with Coach Tim Hennessy of C2X Academy. I saw Tim on TikTok, coaching his wrestling room and talking about taking seven wrestling shots after each practice to get better each day. When I saw that message, I knew this was a person I wished to have on my podcast and learn from. I never expected that we would develop a friendship that would transcend the podcast, including great dinners, meaningful conversations, visits to Rutgers wrestling, giving his daughter an internship, and creating a unique friendship I cherish. Some relationships do not have to be daily. A simple social media post, phone call, or dinner can lift you and inspire you in ways you never could have imagined. Tim has inspired me in many ways, and I'm very grateful to call him a friend and contributor to this project.

To all of the guests, contributors, and stakeholders of the Business Jiu Jitsu project, thank you for all your contributions. There are too many to name, but they include billion-dollar CEOs, world champions, UFC stars, world-class coaches, entrepreneurs, musicians, authors, and many more. Thank you for giving your voice to my podcast and helping me write this book. Every single conversation, whether it was mentioned or made the final cut of this book, informed my thinking and has deeply impacted me. My business has more than doubled since I started this project and is on its way to more growth. I attribute much of this success to immersing myself in conversations that seek success, wealth, and happiness. You get to choose your circle and what gets in between your ears. All the people I spoke with helped me in some way to continue achieving my goals of building my businesses and creating a happy life. Thank you to all of you.

Also, a big thank you to my co-writer, Anastasia Voll, who swooped in to help rescue this project halfway through when it looked like all could have been lost. This book and the stories in it are about overcoming adversity, much like you do in jiu-jitsu when a big, heavy opponent is mounted on top of you. That is what happened halfway through writing this book when my original publisher, who also published my first two books *Coming Into Your Own* and *This Is It*, went bankrupt. Scribe Media took my money, took other authors' money, and through mismanagement went out of business. I had to scramble and assemble a team to get this book published, causing more than a year and a half delay. Thanks to Anastasia, we helped reassemble a team of publishers in Tasfil Publishing, book cover designers, copywriters, editors, publicists, and marketers, and the list goes on. I often said to Anastasia that one of the greatest feelings is being understood by the person you are working with, and many times she blew me away by hearing my stories and helping me turn them into the written words you find on these pages.

Last, but certainly not least, a note for my wife Danielle and my children Axel, Mac, and soon-to-be baby, whom we expect in a few months. This book is an evolving process. As of its publication, I'm 39 years old and have made many mistakes, and each of those mistakes has helped me get to where I am today. It is all for you. I love each of you, and you make it easy to get up and go to work every day. Early mornings and late nights at jiu-jitsu are all for you. Every time I'm at work or go to jiu-jitsu, there's a small bit of guilt about wanting to be with you and wishing I could be with you all the time. Hard work is a gift from G-d; jiu-jitsu or whatever pursuit you wish to devote your life to is also a gift from G-d. When I am doing these things, I do them in order to be a better person, man, husband, and father for you. It is all for you. I do get the added benefit of it also being good for me. When you have a healthy body, mind, and spirit, you can create a happy home and be a better person. I hope that I live up to your ideals and inspire you to become whatever it is you wish to be, as long as it's done with a happy heart, honesty, and integrity. I love you.

About the Author

Jordan Edwards is a partner at Chart Organization, a diversified investment and asset management company founded in 2003 by his father, Glenn Edwards, in honor of Jordan's Grandmother, Norma Chart Edwards. At Chart, Jordan oversees day-to-day operations and acquisitions, working closely with retailers and local businesses across the United States and Canada.

Jordan is also the CEO of Mixology Clothing Company where he is responsible for setting the overall company strategy and overseeing retail, e-commerce, and brand portfolio operations. Mixology has seventeen locations, Shopmixology.com, 450 employees, and over 300,000 active customers.

Finally, Jordan is a Brazilian Jiu Jitsu athlete training under Sensei Nardu Debrah at Budokan Martial Arts Academy. He is co-author with his father of the 2019 book *If You're Waiting for a Sign to Start Your Business, THIS IS IT!* and the host of the @businessjiujitsu podcast.

Jordan graduated from Northeastern University's College of Business Administration, earned his EMBA from Quantic School of Business & Technology, and completed the CORe program at Harvard Business School Online.

"You read the book; now become the book."
– Sensei Nardu

Made in the USA
Middletown, DE
08 September 2024

59849091R00196